CATCH THE VISION OF GOD

Carlo and Michèle Brugnoli

MINERVA PRESS

LONDON

MONTREUX   LOS ANGELES   SYDNEY

ISBN 1 86106 276 1

First Published in English 1997 by
MINERVA PRESS
195 Knightsbridge
London SW7 1RE

French Edition Published 1992 by
Jeunesse en Mission
1261 Burtigny
Switzerland

Printed in Great Britain for Minerva Press

CATCH THE VISION OF GOD

Grateful Acknowledgement

Our warm thanks go to all those who contributed to the realization of this book, in particular Anne Dupont, Jacqueline Tartar, Danièle Imhof, Danièle Stalder and Jean-Paul Rivier, the proof-readers, and Eliane Lack, Tom Bloomer, Marc and Rosine Walter, Philippe and Christine Ziehli, advisors; Joe Portale, reviser; Christine Alexander, English translator. Their collaboration has been invaluable to us.

Contents

Preface

By Floyd McClung

From the very beginning of time, God has desired a relationship with man. He created us in His image with rational, emotional, spiritual, and relational abilities.

God created us for relationship. This great theme runs from the beginning of the Bible to the very end. From the book of Genesis, where He created Adam and Eve and came to walk with them in the garden, to the marriage feast of the Lamb in the book of Revelation where we gather with the Lamb of God for all eternity, the theme of the Bible is relationship.

This God of relationship has invited us to be partners with Him in ministering to the lost and needy people of the world. We do this in many ways and to many people.

Carlo and Michèle Brugnoli have written a book about relationship with our wonderful God. Indeed, we can be 'thrilled' with God because of the greatness of God in His invitation to us to be His partners in reaching our world with the gospel.

Carlo and Michèle teach us how to do that. They teach us about why and how we should pray for the nations, and how we can be in harmony with God's plan for the world. They teach us how we can be a channel for God's love to those who do not know Jesus Christ, and they challenge us to follow through with every person who responds in a positive way.

This is not only a book about a world in need, but a book of hope, a book of compassion, and a book that calls Christians to work together in order that we might be all that God has meant us to be.

This is a book which will build unity for those who hear its message and apply its truths to their hearts. This book is not a rational exercise in theology, but more a book to touch the heart and to change one's life.

I have known Carlo and Michèle for many years, and they live the message they write. I commend Carlo and Michèle and this outstanding book to you. It will not only challenge you, but it will change your life.

January 1992

Introduction

We are probably living in one of the most exciting periods of history. Christianity will have more than two billion adherents by the year 2000, whereas there were little over a quarter of that number a century ago. While Africa had ten million at that time, now, numbers will soon surpass four hundred million! The former USSR, Eastern Europe and Albania, hungry for love and faith after so many years of famine, are now claiming back their right to the 'Good News'. Ideologies pass away, but the wisdom and splendour of the Gospel shine more and more brightly. The Holy Spirit is visiting continent after continent, gathering a harvest of tens of thousands every day, through those who make themselves available to His call. And the time for Europe is coming.

But all these events are woven and formed in the secret place of communion with the God of the universe. His planet-wide projects are realized through the details of the daily life of each of His disciples. He is looking for 'friends' so He can involve them in His plans and equip them with tools as His intercessors and reapers.

Each chapter of this book can be studied independently of the others, so begin with the one that seems most attractive to you! If you read it simply as a novel, you will soon forget it, but if you study it, it could become a launching pad to 'take off' with God. Seize the opportunity!

Chapter I

Around The World with the Holy Spirit

Rarely does the media report to us what God is doing across the continents. Particularly in the West, we are given the impression that Christianity has been overtaken and is losing ground, even if the occasional head of state refers to the Gospel or asks his nation to pray. What is the truth?

In July 1989, four thousand Christian leaders met together in Manila in the Philippines to examine the advance of world evangelization and missions, in this, the end of the second millennium.

Lausanne II, as the international congress was called (referring to the first congress of this type in Lausanne in 1974) brought men and women together, not only from every continent, but from close to one hundred and eighty nations. In respect of peoples represented, it was probably the most diverse gathering in the whole of human history – and it was for the cause of Jesus Christ.

The word of command was this:

Proclaim Christ until He comes!

This implies that:

The whole Church must preach the whole Gospel to the whole world.

Reports in the form of exhibitions, videos and workshops enabled us to gain a better picture of the task already accomplished, and of what is still ahead of us.

Without attempting to summarize those ten days, when fifty renowned speakers took turns to share in plenary sessions, I want to emphasize three foundations with which the Holy Spirit seemed to persistently challenge us and, through us, the believers of the whole world:

1) A biblical, practical, intelligent and charitable *unity* with a view to a credible witness and an unprecedented harvest.

2) An applied *compassion*, the key to reaching whole people groups.

3) A tremendous *hope*, with the day-to-day discovery of the work of God on a planetary scale.

1.1. A Biblical Unity

Have you heard the story of the little girl who was lost in a huge field of corn? Everybody went out searching, all over the field, but nobody found her. After several days without success, they lined themselves up elbow to elbow and systematically made their way across the expanse of the field. They found the child, but by then she was dead...

Unity does not replace work, any more than it would have helped to stand elbow to elbow at the edge of the field and wait! But unity makes work infinitely more effective. I have heard that the rays from a flashlight disappear after a few metres because the photons go in different directions, but with a laserbeam, all the rays converge in one direction and so the rays can reach as far as the moon!

From the eleventh chapter of Genesis onwards, we discover the power of unity: 'If *as one people* speaking the same language they have begun to do this, then *nothing they plan to do* will be impossible for them' (Gen. 11:6).

In contrast, the Head of the Church warns us: 'If a kingdom is divided against itself, that kingdom cannot stand' (Mark 3:24). Yet, as someone has said, 'the Church is the only army in the world that shoots its own soldiers!' Oh that the disciples of Christ at the end of the twentieth century would love each other and fulfil the prayer of our Lord: 'That all of them may be one... so that the world may believe that You have sent Me' (John 17:21).

1.2 Unity Between Developing Countries and the West.

Until 1985, the majority of evangelical Christians[1] were Westerners, but that year the 50% mark was crossed and, by the beginning of the 90s, the proportions had already become 33% to

---

[1]This name is used in its general sense, describing Christians of all denominations who confess Jesus Christ as Lord of their life and the Bible as the Word of God.

66%, that is, two Christians in the developing countries for every one Christian in the West. This does not mean that the Church has diminished in Western countries, but that in many other countries its numbers are exploding.

The Christian world must develop a new mentality: missionary work will no longer be directed exclusively from north to south, but also south to north, east to west, south to west, south to east, etc., forming an international and intercontinental network of Life! It will become less and less uncommon to see an African pastor in France, a Brazilian mission director in Moscow, or a Korean teacher in Washington.

In this vein, the Koreans are preparing to send ten thousand missionaries into the world in the last decade of our millennium. God is endowing His young Church with powerful ministries, which will rekindle the flame of first love and win multitudes to Christ in the countries historically called 'Christianized'. But for this to happen, the older brother in the family of God must welcome and rejoice over the younger brother's growth in potential and maturity... without himself going into retirement!

1.3 Unity in Projects

One day a Christian asked one of the directors of Coca-Cola how they had succeeded in 'cocalizing' the world. "We were organized," he answered. Did not Jesus warn us? 'For the people of this world are more shrewd in dealing with their own kind than are the people of the light.' (Luke 16:8)

Some thirty international projects for the evangelization of our planet were brought into focus during the congress. Each of these aims at one part of the task, with, of course, the possibility of collaboration; for example, someone could be visited by a missionary team, hear a radio broadcast two years later and, sometime after that, see the film *Jesus*. The challenge is for every person to come in contact at least once with the Good News.

But why do all these projects have the year 2000 as their target?

Someone once said, "If you draw your target after you've shot your arrow, you'll always hit the bull's eye!" It takes more courage and humility to dare to fix precise goals at which to aim, than simply to be led by the train of events and see what the outcome is.

A great number of mission organizations and denominations, on every continent and without any consultation with one another, have felt that the Spirit of God was motivating them to mobilize their forces, and to make this last decade of the millennium a decade consecrated to bringing in the harvest.

We must not allow ourselves to get superstitious over the date; it is certainly an anniversary to be celebrated royally, and it would be only normal for the Church to offer its Lord obedience to His last commandment, but the year 2000 will also be a year like all the others, when some will have toothache, some will marry, others will die... a normal year.

Christ will return when the Father judges it to be right; he may come as early as today, or later than we expect. No committee can reproach Him for this! Those who are tempted to make an idol of the year 2000, remember this: Jesus was probably born in the year 'minus 4'. The two thousandth anniversary of His birth would then be in 1996. May the Lord find us busy with the harvest rather than making vain forecasts of the day of His return!

We want to love and proclaim Christ until He comes, with the year 2000 being simply a step on the way. Here are two examples of ways we can do so:

At this point in time, four of the most significant Christian radio networks, ELWA, HCJB ('The Voice of the Andes'), Trans World Radio and Far East Broadcasting Corporation, have together set themselves the objective of proclaiming the Gospel over the airwaves to every people group comprising a million or more, in its mother tongue. The challenge is not really in the technical planning, as shortwave radio can reach around the world several times; it is essentially in the multitude of languages. A miracle is then required for the person who has a radio to be listening at the right moment, on the right frequency, to the transmission aimed at him! Written advertising is not always a possibility.

Campus Crusade has produced the film *Jesus*, drawn entirely from the facts related in the Gospel of Luke, and more than three hundred million people have already seen it. When a film comes out in English, it is one among many others; in contrast, when this film appears in the mother tongue of a small people group, it is a great event. Producers of secular films are mainly concerned with commercial ends; it is therefore a very rare, or even non-existent, occurrence to find films in these languages. So it is that thousands gather together, often in the open air, and discover the words and work of Jesus Christ for the first time. We realize more and more the importance of this ministry, aware that a significant percentage of these people are illiterate and will never be able to read the Gospel.

This organization has subdivided the planet into five thousand regions of about one million inhabitants, and is committed to sending teams to each of the regions, to show the film, by the year 2000.

1.4 Unity in Prayer

Prayer teams from all over the world came to the congress and interceded in relays, twenty-four hours around the clock. In four-hour time slots, these Christians remained before the Spirit of the Lord, praying that His rain would pour down on every aspect of this planet-wide meeting, and would bring forth the fruit expected in the future. I believe it was thanks to that precious commitment of prayer that the congress was not seen as a goal in itself, but as a means to organizing ways to reach every creature with the love of God.

The fervent prayer of the righteous, in unity, enabled the congress to succeed in setting long-term strategies; in 1995 each nation should have its own plan to reach every citizen with the Gospel.

At midnight on July 20th, 1989, a prayer meeting began which, God willing and if we remain faithful, will never stop. In fact, with the aid of differing time zones around the world, this task of intercession is being carried out continuously, in shifts, seven days a week, throughout the year. The main subject for prayer is the Lord's harvest among all people groups. We cannot help but see a connection with the Moravian Brothers, who organized a prayer meeting in the eighteenth century which lasted a hundred years! Many believe that this was the starting point of modern missions.

In chapter three we shall see how we, too, can play a vital role in praying for the nations.

1.5 Unity Between 'Charismatics' and 'Non-Charismatics'

Jesus is not coming to get His brides, but His Bride, for, as someone emphasized, our Lord is not polygamous! The drama is, however, very real when, in a town of fifty thousand inhabitants, one hundred charismatic Christians and one hundred non-charismatic Christians use their energy to criticize each other with arguments, articles and books, sometimes disputes and slander, while allowing tens of thousands to die without Christ! Is this not a scandal and a crime? How will such behaviour be justifiable before the

Bridegroom? These two 'young maidens' may well be virgins, but they are most certainly foolish!

It is not the intention here to neglect sound doctrine, or to concoct a huge doctrinal soup, New Age style. Not at all. But for all of us for whom Jesus Christ is life's centre and who follow Him, it is a duty to respect each other, love each other and support one another in proclaiming the Good News. Denominations then become spiritual families and cease to be clans, or, worse still, entrenched army camps.

1.6 Unity Between Men and Women in Ministry

More than 60% of missionaries in the world are women. In Manila, one thousand places were reserved for them, and not only in the translation booths, hospitality services, or back seats, but also behind the microphones! While the Old Testament recognized them in the roles of queen, judge, prophetess, administrator, counsellor, etc., we see them holding no lesser roles in the Early Church: announcing the Resurrection (John 20:17), accompanying the apostles, training new converts, exercising the gifts of the Spirit (cf. Acts 1:8,14, 2:3, 21:9, 1 Cor. 14:3-4). If the apostle Paul expressed a reserve insofar as the teaching ministry was concerned, before the New Testament was completed, it was certainly not to invalidate all that the Scriptures say from Genesis to Revelation in respect to a woman's place. It is Paul who takes Priscilla and Aquila on to his missionary team, and it is they who, when the apostle left, 'explained to him (Apollos) the way of God more adequately' (Acts 18:18, 26). Again it is Paul who writes to the Galatians to emphasize the grace and value which God gives to each of His children: 'You are all sons of God through faith in Christ Jesus, for all of you who were baptized into Christ have clothed yourselves with Christ. There is neither Jew nor Greek, slave nor free, male nor female, for you are all one in Christ Jesus.' (Gal. 3:26-28).

Each spiritual 'family' has its own convictions concerning the place of women in its midst, but I know of none who refuse to allow its women missionaries to train children and women of all ages as disciples of Christ, and, after all, these two categories represent 72% of the world's population! If that is the case, then on the one hand, no young woman can divest herself of the call of the Master, even within a denomination which is strict on this subject, under the pretext that she cannot exercise her ministry; on the other hand, the denominational leaders must ask themselves the question: are we offering our young women, our wives, our missionaries, the position the apostles would give them, and that which the Holy Spirit would assign to them?

1.7 An Applied Compassion

Who has not heard of 'Smoky Mountain' on the outskirts of Manila? It consists of the refuse of the capital, which forms 'smoking mountains' of rubbish where thousands of people live in the dreadful stench. The poor extract for themselves what other poor people have thrown away, and the children fight with the rats over a piece of rotten fruit or dry bread. Now, was it by chance that this international gathering, first scheduled to take place in Lausanne, then in Singapore, was moved for various practical reasons, finally taking place in the capital of the Philippines?

At the beginning of the congress, the spokeswoman for the President, Mrs Corasón Aquino, welcomed us and expressed her hope that we would also turn our attention to the concrete aspect of a Gospel response to poverty and misery. During the first days of hearing the messages God had put in the hearts of numerous speakers, we saw that hearing what 'the Spirit says to the Church' was not only a natural concern, but a duty.

A couple who were congress delegates were picnicking on a bench in town when a young fourteen year old approached them to beg for his meal.

"We'd like to share our meal with you," they told him, "but don't you have parents?"

"Yes," answered the teenager, "but they took me to a crossroads in town when I was seven, asked me to wait for them there, and never came back..."

"We could become your parents, if you like," the husband answered spontaneously. The eyes of the teenager shone like stars, while the astonished wife, turning to her husband, exclaimed,

"Do you realize what you're saying? The child believes you!"

Yes, he did realize... and almost immediately the same certainty filled the heart of his wife: God was asking them to adopt this child. They took him to a clothing shop and dressed him, according to his own taste, from head to foot. Then they took him to their hotel.

As this couple was part of the intercession groups that had come to Manila especially to pray, the child accompanied them there. His adoptive parents realized that he already knew the Lord. In the course of the week, he was flooded with the love of God, filled with the Spirit and healed of many inner wounds that had come from rejection.

It was at that point that I met him, when his new mother introduced him to us. He was radiant with happiness that his dream had become a reality... And yet, I was confronted with two thoughts, the first being a hard question: what use would this be? What about the thousands of others who were still on the street...? The second was peaceful and affirmed: you see, that is what loving your neighbour as yourself is all about. It was not difficult to discern which was the voice of the Holy Spirit.

What God did for this child, He would want to do for families, for tribes, for nations. How? By pouring His compassion into the heart of every believer, that it might reach the crowds without a shepherd, who are drifting towards destruction.

The Father Who lived in Jesus is the same Who lives in you today. He is no less big, His feelings have not changed, His will is still to do works of compassion. 'It is the Father, living in Me, Who is doing His work.' (John 14:10).

Let us look again at Jesus' description of the Good Samaritan. He is the one who stops, gives his time, dresses the wounds of the needy, lends him his own means of transport, takes him to a hotel, pays for a room for him and guarantees payment of any further expenses. And then Jesus adds, 'Go and do likewise' (Luke 10:25-37).

Jesus is this Good Samaritan *par excellence*, and when his disciple Philip, asked Him to show them the Father, Jesus gave him this now-famous response, 'Don't you know Me, Philip, even after I have been among you such a long time? Anyone who has seen Me has seen the Father... Don't you believe that I am in the Father, and that the Father is in Me?' (John 14:8-10).

We have so often put in opposition what the Holy Spirit puts in parallel, opting either for the proclamation of the Gospel or for compassion toward the poor of all categories, while the Master, far from denying one aspect of the Gospel for another, showed so clearly that love in action was the key to penetrating hearts with the Word, the source of salvation.

The works of the righteous were not initiated by the International Red Cross, the UN, nor yet Civil Rights, although all these movements have praiseworthy aspects, but it is in fact our Lord Himself who assigns them to us:

- I was hungry and *you* gave Me something to eat.
- I was thirsty and *you* gave Me something to drink.
- I was a stranger and *you* invited Me in.
- I was naked and *you* clothed Me.
- I was sick and *you* looked after Me.
- I was in prison and *you* came to visit Me (Matt. 25:35-36).

As never before, a large number of those four thousand Christian leaders understood that God was again giving to His children a mandate of compassion capable of opening up whole people groups to the kingdom of God.

The fulfilment of Christ's last command, 'Go, make disciples of all nations,' cannot take place without the active participation of every Christian, demonstrating in everyday life the works of the righteous and the compassion of God toward those with whom He has daily contact.

Our job usually takes up 50 to 75% of our waking hours. In the hand of God, a job can become a vocation, light and flavour in a society with little trust, kindness or compassion.

Sometimes we so spiritualize 'full-time work' that the reason for which God has given us our profession is riddled with doubt, even contempt, to the point where it seems a dead work to us. In Manila, one of the speakers in a plenary session asked all those who had been converted through a layperson to stand, and the vast majority rose! How could an evangelist or pastor get into your office, school or factory to preach the Gospel? And supposing he did manage, it would only be for a very brief visit...

We must grasp the fact that God saves far more people through friendships and relationships, in all jobs and professions, than through Gospel 'professionals'. Both are necessary, but let us stop thinking the grass is greener on the other side of the fence. Of course, Christ can change our profession, but He can also give it its true dimensions. Let us not forget that, being in the perfect will of God, Jesus spent about eighteen years practising the trade of a carpenter.

The financially poor are numerous, but those who are poor in relationships, poor in having a reason to live, poor because divorced, rejected, aborted, seduced, betrayed, used, disabled, are legion. In other words, the poor of Calcutta need the compassion of Mother Teresa, but the people in your circle of contact need yours, today.

It is on this daily compassion, whether exercised or not, that the evangelization of our planet largely depends.

1.8 A Tremendous Hope

The information below is simply a representation of the multitude of reports, studies and consultations that took place each day. My aim is to draw you into what filled the hearts of the congress delegates, so that you, too, might be stirred with the desire to better know the work of our Father Who has never ceased to love our universe.

South America

From the three hundred and fifty workshops offered, we had the opportunity to attend eight at the most, in the time allotted. I chose to listen to the testimony of Pastor Omar Ca Brera of Santa Fé, Argentina.

When he arrived in his new parish fourteen years previously, it consisted of fourteen members. He was immediately informed that it was useless to evangelize a hostile population, locked into a conglomeration of superstitions and religions. His role would be to take care of his sheep, and nothing more.

This man disobeyed royally, hallelujah! He began an arduous task of persevering sowing. The population responded with indifference, mockery and persecutions, just as he had been told. But the evangelizing went on, night after night, for five hundred and four evenings in a row!

By the end of this first series of meetings, two to three hundred people were being baptized every week! Today, this fellowship numbers no less than one hundred thousand active members and is thus the third largest local church in the whole world!

In 1980, evangelical Christians would wrap their Bibles in newspaper to avoid being jeered at. Today it is not unusual to see among the crowd in a bus twenty or thirty people with Bibles under their arms. The media, completely closed in the past, now telephones pastors and offers them free broadcasting, five hours at a time.

Nightclubs ask for the Gospel to be preached on their premises and numbers of people are converted.

There are growing churches of twenty, thirty, fifty thousand members. 'The strong man' is bound, the veil of unbelief has been torn down and great crowds are entering into a living relationship with God.

Simultaneously, the work of the Holy Spirit is growing in a number of surrounding countries, such as Chile, where 25% of the population has already been born again. In Santiago the Assemblies of God alone number some two thousand local churches.

In Colombia, where 1% of the population is involved in drug trafficking, the evangelical Protestant churches have grown from three thousand members to two million in the last thirty years!

South American Christians are praying for one third of the population to be born again before the year 2000, and for two hundred and fifty thousand local churches to be established! At the present growth rate, this goal is a real probability, as it would require each church to subdivide or reproduce itself only once.

All of this further translates itself into a development of the continent's missionary responsibility. In 1980, Latin America could count about one thousand one hundred missionaries sent out; eight years later the number had already almost tripled to over three thousand, and now...?

I was in Dakar, Senegal, when I heard that twenty-two Brazilian missionaries had just arrived at the airport. I also knew that they had one-way tickets to the neighbouring country of Guinea Bissau. But what connection is there between that country and Brazil? The Portuguese language, of course!

The goal of these missionaries? To make of this nation a disciple of Jesus Christ! This radical approach can surprise, even offend, our Western mentality, but is it not exactly what Jesus commanded us to do? Is it not the ultimate goal of every missionary? Difficulties, persecutions and tests without number neither change nor dilute the command of the Master. In no way would I want to discourage, with pessimistic rationalism, this new missionary thrust of our brothers and sisters from developing countries. On the contrary, I want to rejoice with all my heart.

Let's Stay In Africa

In the year 1900, Zaïre's population included 1.4% Christians of whatever leaning; in 1990, this number had risen to 90%, of which about 18% are evangelicals! Of course, the church is young and it will still take time for the Christian ethic to impregnate the mentality and the country's institutions, just as it did in the 'old continent'. In this respect, Scripture Union has cast a 'chain of honesty' into the country, just as it has in Madagascar and Peru. Members of the Bible Society involved there command a growing trust and respect. As they refuse all dishonest gain, they are often forced to find supplementary work in order to survive.

Up to this point, Zaïre has already sent out more than two thousand inter-tribal or international missionaries.

Burkina Faso, for a long time considered one of the poorest countries in the world, has also begun to send out its own missionaries. These are supported, both spiritually and financially, by the Christians of the country. The Assemblies of God have grown from a hundred and twenty thousand to three hundred thousand members in the last few years. A spirit of prayer inspires these Christians who, thanks to a common task and good planning in the area of Bible schools and pastors' training, expect to grow to one million between now and the year 2000.

In Nigeria, the seventeen million evangelical Christians continue to increase. One 'mother' church of fifty thousand members now has more than a thousand 'daughters', that is, fellowships of believers springing from the original nucleus. This vast nation of more than one hundred and fifteen million will have sent out, on its own and with little effort, three thousand missionaries!

The evangelist Reinhard Bonnke, for example, held a six-day campaign in Kaduna, in the centre of the country, and two hundred thousand cards showing decisions for Christ were filled in! In those six days, more than one and a half million people (five hundred thousand in one evening alone) attended the crusade.

In connection with this evangelism team, it is not rare today to see more than half of a town, even a large one, all go on one evening to hear the Good News. This was the case in Ouagadougou (Burkina Faso), where two hundred and fifty thousand inhabitants out of four hundred thousand attended the last meeting, and again in Lomé (Togo), where two hundred thousand attended out of three hundred thousand inhabitants.

Compare this with your own town or village! God is not a big God in Africa and a 'little' God in Europe – Europe's turn will also come!

In almost all of Africa below the Sahara, there is a tremendous spiritual thirst; we live in a time of exceptionally widespread harvest, perhaps unique in the history of mankind. However, let us not forget that in Burkina Faso, only thirty years ago, evangelistic efforts were ended with a shower of stones, and that it took the first missionaries in Togo eighteen years before seeing their first convert...

Before leaving the African continent, I want to mention the Comore Islands in the Indian Ocean (between the island of Madagascar and Mozambique). It was in 1973 that the first Comorian was converted. In 1980, there were thirty. One of them, invited to 'Lausanne II', related the following facts to us. Because of his faith in Christ, this disciple was violently persecuted, then condemned to death. Whilst awaiting his execution, he was locked in a special cell where it was impossible either to stand, sit, or even lie down. This torture lasted three months, before he was once more summoned before the authorities. During the proceedings, he fell to his knees and cried out to God. The judge, thinking he was mad, sent him back to his own village chained to a policeman. His first convert was the policeman himself! At the time of his sharing this martyr's testimony with us, one hundred and thirty-seven people from his village had already become Christians!

Asia

The gigantic size of this continent, comprising well over half the world's population, overwhelms us... but that is not the case with the Lord, Who said, 'Be fruitful and multiply; fill the earth and subdue it' (Gen. 1:28). He is the same God, Who moves by His Holy Spirit, that the greatest possible number might be saved and share in His eternal glory.

When we look at a crowd of Chinese children, all we see is a thousand faces as like one another as photocopies. But God sees in each face a life unique and different from the one next to it, with its own story, its large or small troubles, its prayers, dreams, qualities and weaknesses; He even distinguishes between each thought and every hair on his head. This child is as precious in His eyes as Jesus Himself, and He has a plan, to offer this child, one day, a personal relationship with Him.

If God is like this, we can expect Him to act on a scale as large as this continent. It is in fact what the missiologists have confirmed in the last few years, discovering that every forty-five days up to one million people are converted in China!

How do we interpret this figure? On one hand, it means that, even at this pace, it would take one hundred and twenty-three years to see a billion conversions (a thousand times forty-five days). On the other hand, we need to grasp the fact that never, in the whole history of the Church, has there been a harvest parallel to this. In comparison, the great revivalist Charles Finney saw from the beginning to the end of his ministry, half a million people come to Christ.

Another landmark to remember is the famous Welsh Revival at the beginning of the twentieth century, when a hundred thousand were converted in six months. With good reason, this was considered altogether exceptional. We can therefore rejoice without reserve, even while knowing that the work and the battles are still great.

Let us look at the example of the Chinese Christian who was tortured in the most vile manner: his head put in a noose, his feet barely resting on a stool, his hands tightly bound. The intention was that, when exhausted, he would sink down and so be hanged.

Without giving him a single drop of water, two guards awaited the moment for two hours... then two days... then seven days. This believer longed many a time to give up the struggle, but miraculously God enabled him to hold out for thirteen days, during which he was a witness for Christ before his tormentors! On the thirteenth day the sky darkened and a storm broke out, and finally the man lost consciousness and collapsed. He was thought to be dead when the guards, extremely upset, shook him to revive him as he lay on the ground. At the same moment, a flash of lightning completely severed the rope that was intended to finish off this wreckage of a human being. This new divine intervention overcame the sarcasm and unbelief of the two torturers. It is sometimes at such a price that the Church in China advances... but it is advancing!

In Seoul, South Korea, the largest local church is to be found, with more than seven hundred thousand active members. In this city of ten million people there are many other evangelical fellowships, many of which have tens of thousands of members.

Pray that the fear of the Lord will remain strong in the hearts of all these Christians, for they are being tested in a way that is far from easy: the test of success! In fact, if nothing grieves the Holy Spirit and the wind of revival continues at the present pace, 75% of the country's population could be born again by the year 2000.

Do we have examples of such phenomena in the history of the Church or in the Bible? The city of Rochester, USA, experienced a revival movement where eighty thousand out of one hundred thousand inhabitants experienced profound conversion through the ministry of Charles Finney. The atmosphere of the town was affected for years: prisons were empty, lawyers and judges out of work, alcohol retailers bankrupt, brothels closed down! The phenomenon was so powerful that at certain campaign meetings, not a single person could be found who was not bowing the knee before Christ!

In New Testament times, we read in the Acts of the Apostles: 'As Peter travelled about the country, he went to visit the saints in Lydda. There he found a man named Aeneas, a paralytic who had been bedridden for eight years. "Aeneas," Peter said to him, "Jesus Christ heals you. Get up and take care of your mat." Immediately Aeneas got up. *All* those who lived in *Lydda* and *Sharon* saw him and *turned* to the Lord.' (Acts 9:32-35)

The most well-known example in the Old Testament would be that of Nineveh, a tremendously widespread city, according to the text, and consisting of a hundred and twenty thousand people. Following the prophet's warning, the inhabitants took the Word of God seriously. The king commanded that every person cry out to God with all his strength and repent of every evil act and the violence of which he was guilty. Then God 'had compassion and did not bring upon them the destruction He had threatened' (cf. Jon. 3:3,5,8,10).

We know that the new covenant is superior to the old, and that in the last days, beginning at Pentecost, the Holy Spirit will be poured out on all flesh. It is therefore legitimate to expect an exceptional harvest, even if the powers of hell are breaking loose at the same time!

The return of Hong Kong to China in 1997 is imminent. From 14th to 18th November 1990, the Christians there organized an evangelistic campaign with Billy Graham that was relayed by satellite to more than thirty countries. One hundred and twenty-three thousand churches prepared counsellors! Millions heard the Gospel translated simultaneously into forty-five languages.

Yes, God knows the means to reach Asia, and He has not let go of the helm!

There is the little Korean lady, also, who was sent as a missionary to Japan. On her arrival in Tokyo, she locked herself into a hotel room for twenty-one days of fasting and prayer. This somewhat revolutionary missionary approach bore its fruit. While Japanese churches often count about forty members, this woman of God saw the largest church in Japan brought to birth, consisting of five thousand members in 1989. These Christians are praying for the conversion of ten million Japanese by the year 2000!

In 1965, there were only five known Christians in the small Hindu kingdom of Nepal. In spite of the fact that for a long time the government has forbidden any conversion to Christianity, there are forty to fifty thousand Christians today, shared between one hundred and fifty churches. Who but God can multiply a people group by ten thousand in less than thirty years?

Eastern Europe And the Former USSR

The events of history seem to be gaining speed; almost every day brings a piece of news more astonishing than the one before it.

In response to many years of intercession by millions of Christians both within and without these countries, the stamp of an immense, divine movement can be discerned, and a mobilization of the heavenly hosts. Look at these hopeful signs:

USSR, 1989: On a square in Leningrad, now Saint Petersburg, ten thousand people quietly watch a Youth With A Mission team give a presentation of the Gospel. The 'King's Kids' are welcomed in Soviet youth camps. A Christian witness goes out on national television...

Former USSR, 1991: teams testify that, among daily audiences of one thousand five hundred people, more than half respond when an appeal for conversion is given.

The spiritual thirst is such that the Bible Society believes thirty million Bibles will need to be provided by 1993.

Hungary: The city of Budapest witnessed twenty thousand conversions in a single day at the Billy Graham campaign, which was attended by eighty thousand people. Imagine the tears of joy in the eyes of those who had just lived through more than forty years of persecution and underground Christianity...

How much longer will it be before we can report on crowds pressing in for drops of living water in Romania, Poland and Albania?

And The West?

In spite of the wait for revival, there are still encouraging events taking place, like the hundred thousand decisions for Christ in the Billy Graham campaign in 1989 in England. Invited to Manila as a guest of honour, Mr Graham gave up the trip to remain where he was, as the move of God was so powerful throughout the two hundred-odd spots where the campaign was being simultaneously transmitted.

In a similar campaign three years before, 68% of those who had filled in decision cards were still faithful and involved in local churches a year later. This is a testimony to an exemplary follow-up programme of which I have several times been a witness.

It is true that I have often cited this evangelist who has so marked our generation, for I do not think it wise to appreciate such a ministry only after it is gone, an error we make too often. Billy Graham has proclaimed the Gospel to more people than anyone else has ever done; he has remained humble and faithful in a fruitful ministry lasting more than half a century. He was the inspiration behind the Lausanne movement, and yet, because of the great harvest in England and his own fatigue, he gave up coming to Manila.

I hope and pray regularly that God will lend us this evangelist for many years yet, and that millions will continue to enter the Kingdom through this precious ministry; but could it be that, through his last-minute cancellation, the Lord wanted to teach us to continue the work together, even without Billy Graham?

Looking at England once again, it is expected that by the year 2000 every inhabitant would have been able to hear the Gospel five times in various ways. Because of this, but also through praise and intercession marches uniting tens of thousands of Christians, this country could become, as in centuries past, a hotbed of revival for Europe.

Another demonstration was the Torch Run. At Easter 1988, on the Mount of Ascension, Jerusalem, where Jesus' disciples heard His last words, a flame was lit. Thomas Wang, then president of the Lausanne movement, Loren Cunningham, founder of Youth With A Mission and initiator of the Run, as well as other leaders, were present to symbolically pass on the baton of missions and world evangelization to the next generation.

From this point of departure, teenagers responding to the call of God ran, torch in hand, in every continent. In July 1989, five hundred thousand had already taken part, thus demonstrating the reality of the new missionary generation.

Thomas Wang was also there to welcome a delegation of the runners at the opening meeting in Manila. Throughout their courses across the whole world, the Gospel was proclaimed, prayer groups were formed, young people committed themselves to Christ. In the French-speaking part of Switzerland, three thousand youths were mobilized, and more than two hundred towns and villages were visited, with conversions in every canton, as first-fruits.

1.9 The Advance of the Gospel in the World, and Challenges Before Us

At the time of the first Pentecost, the Holy Spirit was poured out on a hundred and twenty people. The world then had about one hundred and sixty million inhabitants, which means that, before Peter's sermon, there was less than one Christian for every one million non-Christians.

On the evening of that first day of the Church, the three thousand new converts and the disciples together still represented only 0.002% of the world's population, there being only one Christian for every fifty thousand non-Christians!

Since then, the proportion of disciples has not ceased to grow and, because of this, the number of people to evangelize, per witnesses to Christ, has diminished through the centuries. *Where do we stand today?*

Non-Christians And Nominal[2] Christians, Per Disciple[3]

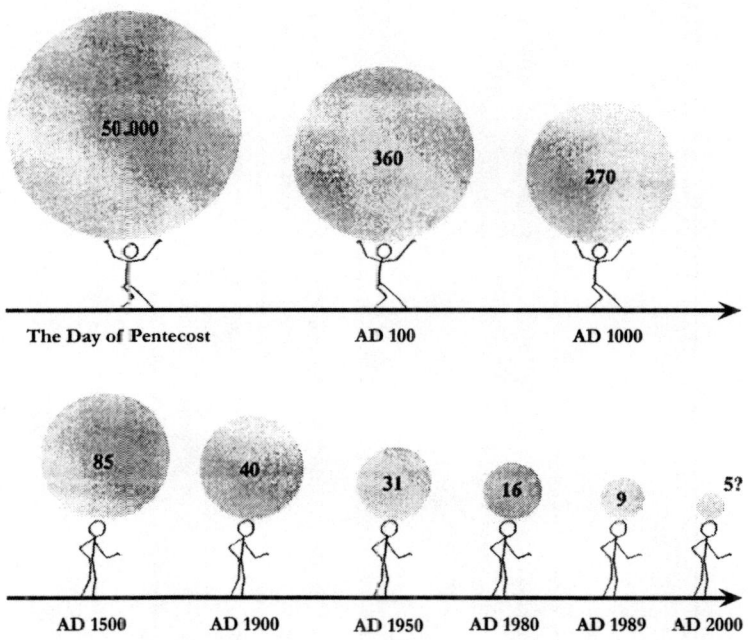

This chart shows how, in the course of two thousand years of Christianity, the people of God have multiplied and taken on their missionary responsibility. Today, if every believer evangelized nine different people, every person on the globe would hear the Good News.

---

[2] To the question, 'Are you a Christian?' these answered in the affirmative, but their adherence is essentially a socio-cultural one.

[3] Denotes a Christian (of any denomination) who claims Jesus as Lord and participates in the Great Commission (Matt. 28:19-20, Mark 16:15). Some charts published differ slightly as they do not count nominal Christians, but show only the proportion of non-Christians to disciples. Source: Centre for World Mission, Mission Frontiers, March 1989.

The Finishable Task!

Year (A.D.)	Total World Population (Millions)	People who do not claim to be Christians (Millions)	People who call themselves Christians (Millions)	Great Commission Christians (out of Col #4) (Millions)	Non-Christians per Believer	Unreached People groups	Congregations per Unreached People group
1	2	3	4	5	6	7	8
100	181	180	1	0.5	1:360	60,000	1:12
1000	270	220	50	1	1:270	50,000	1:5
1500	425	344	81	5	1:85	44,000	1:1
1900	1,620	1,062	558	40	1:40	40,000	10:1
1950	2,504	1,650	854	80	1:31	24,000	33:1
1980	4,458	3,020	1,433	275	1:16	17,000	162:1
1989	5,160	3,438	1,722	500	1:9	12,000	416:1
2000	6,260	4,130	2,130	1000	1:5	0?	?

The figures in the first four columns of this chart are taken directly from the World Christian Encyclopaedia; the fifth and sixth show the missionary force in relation to the actual challenge. The seventh column records the number of unreached people groups (often many within one nation). The eighth column compares the number of active churches in relation to unreached people groups.

Note: We are referring to the definitions of the Lausanne Committee for World Evangelization (LCWE) for the term 'Great Commission Christians', which denotes those believers who take seriously the last command of Jesus Christ to go into all the world and proclaim the Gospel (Matt. 28:19-20). Columns 1 to 4: World Christian Encyclopaedia, David Barrett. Columns 5 to 8: LCWE Statistics Task Force.

(Source: Centre for World Mission, Mission Frontiers, March 1989.)

Graph Full Of Hope!

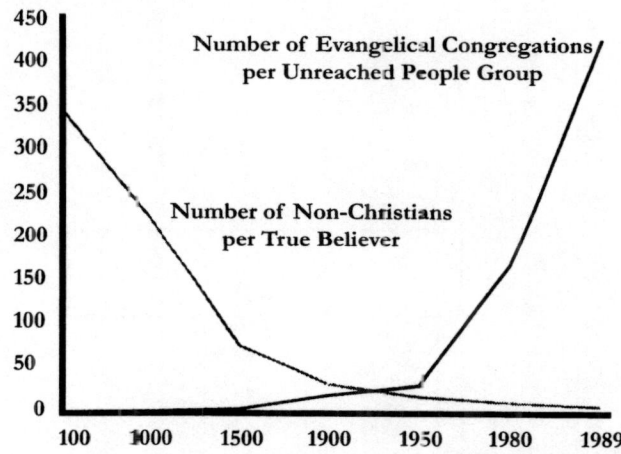

Here we see the incredible possibilities which are ours today, to obey the command and accomplish the mandate that Christ has given to His Church: in the year 100, each church community would have had to reach, alone, twelve people groups, while today close to five hundred churches could collaborate to reach one single people group! It must be possible, even for a group that is hostile and far away!

In other words, it would be sufficient for one local church out of five hundred to send missionaries to an unreached people group in order for the Gospel to reach every people group on the earth! Will my church get involved? Paul made it a point of honour to proclaim Christ where He had not yet been proclaimed (Rom. 15:20).

(Source: Centre for World Mission, Mission Frontiers, March 1989.)

The twelve thousand unreached people groups, representing more than a billion inhabitants, have been completely neglected until now. All the research carried out is seeking to help missions and denominations to put a stop to this deficiency, drawing attention to the ethnic groups who are ignorant of salvation in Jesus Christ, like the Macedonians in the time of Paul. These people groups are mainly concentrated in Africa and Asia, between the tenth and fortieth latitudes north of the equator. The area is thus called the '10-40 Window'.

10 – 40 Window

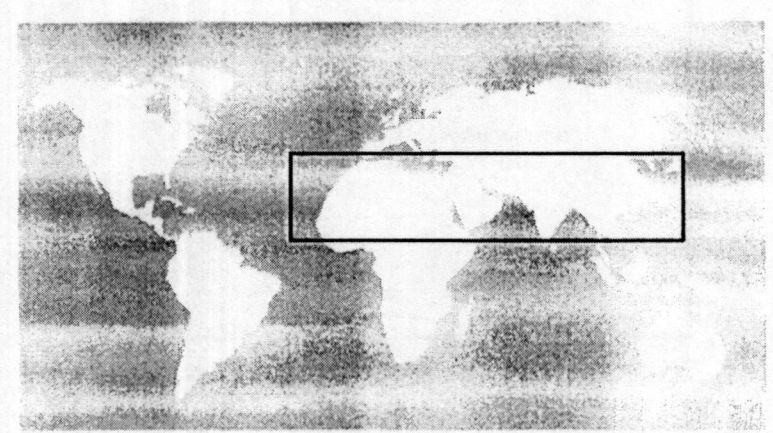

DETACHABLE PAGE TO RECORD
PERSONAL REFLECTION

Summary of Chapter I, Around The World With The Holy Spirit

- Unity:

1. What steps shall I take to contribute to the unity of my church?

a) _____

b) _____

c) _____

2. In my town or village?

a) _____

b) _____

c) _____

- Compassion:

Who is my neighbour (name)? _____

How can I lovingly respond to his needs? _____

_____

_____

- Hope:

What information has strengthened my hope today?

a) _____

b) _____

c) _____

What are the changes this will produce in my life?

a) _____

b) _____

c) _____

Almost five hundred Christian fellowships per unreached people group exist today. However, very few are concerned with concretely accomplishing the last commandment.

How can I personally get involved? Bible study? Research? Missionary prayer group? _____

When shall begin? _____

What is my prayer in the face of the challenge of world evangelization? _____

_____

Chapter II
Sharing God's Passion

When God began to speak with Abram, His friend, He had to share the passion of His heart with him: 'I want all the families of the earth to be blessed through your descendants' (cf. Gen. 12:3). Well, why not bless a few families – but all families? And would we not have shot back the sceptical retort, 'Is that really biblical?' For 'all' implies my family, meaning that old unbelieving uncle, that dreadful cousin, that niece who is so full of faults and... my husband, or... my wife! It also means the Browns, the Joneses, and the next-door neighbours...

Later David, filled with the Holy Spirit, proclaimed, 'Praise the Lord, *all* you nations; extol Him, *all* you peoples' (Ps. 117:1).

Before leaving His disciples, Jesus took care to underline one last time that the heart of God has always embraced *all* His creation: 'This is what is written: The Christ will suffer and rise from the dead on the third day, and repentance and forgiveness of sins will be preached in His name to *all* nations, beginning at Jerusalem" (Luke 24:46-47). It was then as it is today, that only His friends understand the weight of these words.

Shall we look also at the four 'all's which Jesus leaves with us in a parallel passage? '*All* power is given unto Me in heaven and in earth. Go ye therefore, and teach *all* nations, baptizing them in the name of the Father, and of the Son, and of the Holy Ghost: teaching them to observe *all* things whatsoever I have commanded you: and lo, I am with you *always [all the days]*, even unto the end of the world" (Matt. 28:18-20, King James Version). Never could a head of state, nor even an archangel, make such a pronouncement. This means one of two things: either it is outlandish pretentiousness which will be totally ineffective, or it is the incomparable word of command for all Christendom of every era until the return of Christ.

Every reader must make his choice, for if this word is true, it is *the* principal reason for the present existence of this planet and, consequently of his own existence!

Yes, all the authority of Jesus Christ spreads throughout all the centuries, that His liberating truth may reach all men. It is the most powerful sentence that the earth has ever heard since its creation!

2.1 Being Excited Until His Return

On what criteria does God in His sovereignty decide the time of His Son's return, and announce it?

False messiahs, wars and rumours of wars, dissensions on family, national and international levels, famines, earthquakes, persecutions, hatred and betrayals, loss of faith, false prophets and love grown cold... these are the signs of the times announcing His return (cf. Mark 13, Matt. 24). Jesus revealed these things to us at several different times, and even reproached people for not recognizing them. But is this a truly complete list? No, a thousand times no! Listen again to the Lord:

'And the gospel must first be preached to *all* nations.' (Mark 13:10), 'And this gospel of the kingdom will be preached in the *whole world* as a testimony to *all* nations, and *then* the end will come.' (Matt. 24:14.). So, the disciples must understand and obey the command in order for this last sign to be accomplished. Jesus will come back when the work is done.

It is also in this context, as if to emphasize its weight and significance, that Jesus says again, 'Heaven and earth will pass away, but My words will never pass away' (Matt. 24:35).

Reinhard Bonnke, the evangelist, spoke a very simple truth, but a truth charged with significance: 'We have only one generation to reach this generation.' Why? Because the Good News cannot be preached to those not yet born, or to those already dead! Consequently, in each generation the work must be redone.

Further evidence for this is that all men alive today on the face of the earth, Christian and non-Christian, will be dead in a little over a century. There will therefore have to be, at least once in the history of the Church, a generation that announces the Good News to all people and thus obeys the words of Jesus to the full. What are we going to do?

We can leave the challenge to our children, or to our grandchildren, but we can also take Jesus at His word and believe that His command is not only wise, but attainable.

The generation which obeys Him totally will also see the perfect manifestation of His absolute authority, according to His own expression that 'all power has been given to Me', the weight of His glory, His purifying holiness, His signs and wonders, His love and unlimited power turning entire cities and people groups upside-down, and so preparing His glorious 'Bridal Church', without stain or wrinkle, but holy and blameless for Him, the Bridegroom (Eph. 5:27).

If, between the *ascension* and the *return* of Jesus, the main vocation of all Christians is really to bless all the families of the earth, then this truth must perforce be visible in the New Testament.

2.2 Listening to His Word

The entire sum of the words Jesus left us could be put together in a mere fifty pages! Yet they have had more influence on humanity than millions of other volumes. To those few pages Jesus committed an impressive number of teachings, particularly parables, concerning us specifically. Here is a brief summary:

- Parable of the talents (Matt. 25:14-30)
- Parable of the coins (Luke 19:11-27)
- Parable of the vine (Mark 12:1-12)

The principle here is simple: a king (or master) entrusts his goods to his servants, goes away, and returns after a certain time to judge the diligence of his overseers. Who is this king, if not Jesus Himself? Who are his servants, if not you and I? What are these goods, that can be hidden, or shared for multiplication or bearing fruit, if not the Gospel, the key to the Kingdom of God?

Other parables enlighten us on the Enemy who opposes the King's plan of blessing, seeking to prevent the spreading of the Good News:

- Parable of the weeds sown at night (Matt. 13:24-30)
- Parable of the seed eaten by birds (Luke 8:4-15)
- Parable of the thief and murderer (John 10:10)

There are also some regarding human weakness, stubbornness and sin, which dishearten the King and grieve His servants:

- Parable of the great feast where all the guests have an excuse

for not coming (Matt. 22:1-14)
- Parable of the lost sheep (Luke 15:4-7)
- Parable of the lost coin (Luke 15:8-10)
- Parable of the prodigal son (Luke 15:11-32)

Still other parables are addressed to the servants, the salt of the earth and light of the world, exhorting them to be vigilant:

- Parable of the wise and foolish virgins (Matt. 25:1-13)
- Parable of the house on the rock or the sand (Matt. 7:24-27)

Happy are those who watch, obey, remain faithful and persevere for the King!

We end this brief summary by mentioning the righteous judgement of God:

- Parable of the fish sorted out on the shore (Matt. 13:47-50)
- Picture of the sheep and the goats (Matt. 25:31-46)

It is impossible to call this last picture a parable when it refers to the last judgement. The same applies when Jesus lifts the veil from the 'after-death' experience of the rich man and Lazarus (Matt. 16). For every effort which God employs, His immense compassion and His age-old patience cannot annul His justice, whatever the cry of the universalists.

Let us grasp two things from this short survey:

1) Jesus enlightens us on:
- The meaning of existence.
- The true goal of life.
- The corrupting plans of the devil.
- God's activity and involvement, in contrast with...
- Man's lack of concern and sin.
- The importance of man's choice and its eternal consequences.

2) These precious truths will be understood only by His friends or those who wish to become His friends. Neither His sympathizers, nor His admirers, nor even those who, though studying His words, twist and dilute the truth, will grasp their gravity or decisive reality. All this leads us to the crucial point, the *salvation or eternal loss of the human being*.

While in the Old Testament God reveals to us His plan of love for the world, in the New Testament Jesus explains the strategy, means and conditions for it. His life, His teaching and His death on the cross were all leading to this one goal: salvation of the greatest number, the first blessing on which all others depend.

From then on, it has been possible for all men to receive forgiveness, know God as a Father, and freely receive new, eternal life. All that remains to be done is to proclaim it, after having been clothed with His power. It was in this same way that the first disciples were thrown into the midst of the action.

2.3 The First Disciples Get Excited

All the same, as we know, the apostle Peter really needed quite a push (with visions and divine appointments), before he accepted going to the home of a non-Jew (and non-Christian) to announce this Good News! In Acts 10 and 11 we see that the early church of Jerusalem was also not exactly enthusiastic at first over the apostle's evangelizing adventure. But after having heard his explanations, they all finally understood, accepted and rejoiced with heaven.

The change, or rather the opening of the apostle's heart, took some work, but it was none the less total and absolute. In fact it is he who later wrote to the first Christians that the reason for the patience of God is that He is 'not wanting anyone to perish, but *everyone* to come to repentance'. Then he adds this magnificent phrase: 'Look forward to the day of God and speed its coming' (cf. 2 Pet. 3:9-12). It was to this that he dedicated his life, according to Jesus' prophecy. 'Don't be afraid; from now on you will be a fisher of men' (Luke 5:10).

It is impossible to study the life of Paul in any depth here, nevertheless, through the circumstances of his conversion, which marked every day of his ministry, we discover a Christianity which has nothing to do with religion, and which demonstrates the exceptional character of his understanding of the plan of God for humanity. He did not hesitate to live and die for the 'treasure', the 'pearl of great price' which he had found.

In response to much questioning, and also because of the deviations of the Corinthians, Paul puts into writing the first epistle of which we know. Confronting the slander concerning him, that is rife like a venom infecting the strong ties that unite him to his converts, the apostle sees he must open a private window into the very basis of his motivations. How can he defend his ministry without appearing pretentious? How can he protect these Christians from the false prophets?

42

In 1 Cor. 9:19-23, he says: 'I make myself a slave to everyone, *to win as many as possible.* To the Jews I became like a Jew, *to win the Jews.* To those under the law I became like one under the law... *so as to win those under the law.* To those not having the law I became like one not having the law... *so as to win those not having the law.* To the weak I became weak, *to win the weak.* I have become all things to all men, *so that by all possible means I might save some.* I do *all* this for the sake of the gospel, that I may share in its blessings.'

Let us point out at once that this passage is not written by an evangelist, lest many think it applicable only to those specifically involved in that ministry. No, the author of this masterly declaration is a true apostle. If some still doubted that the need to possess these same motivations is valid for every Christian, Paul exhorts us twice more in the same epistle, to be imitators of him, as he imitates Christ (4:16, 11:1). He sends the same message to the Philippians: 'Whatever you have learned or received or *heard* from me, or *seen* in me – put it into practice. And the God of peace *will be with you*" (Phil. 4:9). The apostle therefore takes extreme care to communicate, as clearly as he possibly can, a lifestyle that has as its only goal the salvation of as many as possible, and the giving of the Gospel to all people of every language and every culture, to all families and all individuals.

Billy Graham once said, 'There are in life certain minutes that are worth thousands of eternities...' Such a minute has perhaps come for you at this very moment. In fact, to obey God, to serve Him willingly and embrace His thousand-year perspective, is not an optional pastime for unemployed Christians, but a radical choice which will change your life and consequently the present and eternal lives of hundreds, if not thousands, of others.

Could we but find today:

– Apostles, missionaries, Christian leaders of the same mould as Paul, on fire for the salvation of as many as possible, and dedicating their whole organization, their committees, their staff, their projects, their finances, their vehicles and their computers to this goal!

– Pastors like Timothy who, with radiant lives, have vision for the growth of the Church, train up ardent Christians, preach the Word both in season and out of season, and do the work of evangelists. (cf. 2 Tim. 4:1-5)

– 'Normal' Christians, with no training or special diploma, whose lives infect and impregnate their environment with their own consuming desire for the evangelization of the world (John 2:17).

The age-old trap of the devil is to give Christians such a narrow and limited picture of what evangelism is that they no longer feel it is their concern, thinking that there are the 'initiated ones' on the one hand, and the 'exempted ones' on the other. The devil was a liar from the start, and will remain so until the end, with the goal of losing, in the strict sense, a maximum number of human beings created in the image of God and for whom Christ gave His life. Yes, this seduction is a tragedy that will have eternal consequences.

2.4 Sharing God's Passion in Your Workplace

There are a thousand and one professions that are useful and precious before God. Take the example of a water engineer. In this decade, our planet is going to need three times the amount of drinking water than what is now available. Who will rise up to give drink to those who are thirsty? Of course, the engineer could close his eyes and ears and simply let people die of thirst or disease, or comfort himself with the type of theology that says: it has to happen like this, the world is in a bad state, there is nothing that can be done… But he could also dedicate his profession to this problem, and see entire peoples turn to the One who inspires such vocations. This has already happened in the course of history, and still today determines the destiny of many nations.

Imagine if, one day, our local hospital is looking for a surgeon, and the best one available is a Christian filled with the Spirit of God. And if the same thing happened when the *Herald Tribune*, *The Economist* or *Young Africa* is wanting a journalist or a correspondent; and again for the garage man on the corner, the fridge repairman and the window washer… Would it be so amazing? Is this not the way God has 'salted' the earth for millenniums? Was not Joseph the best prime minister that Pharaoh could find? Daniel, the best counsellor in Babylon? Was not Nehemiah in the service of the king? And Esther the queen of a kingdom that spread from India to Ethiopia? Would the new covenant be less glorious than the old? Would God now have more limited plans? Should Christians withdraw from the world, like a packet of salt set beside a tasteless soup or, under pretext of humility, melt anonymously into the crowd?

Too many sincere Christians think that giving a drink to someone has nothing to do with evangelism, and neither has repairing a car, bringing up a child, washing the floor, managing the finances of a society, inventing... when in fact everything influences this one essential. The question God has for us today is not, 'What is your profession?' but, 'Why, and for what purpose, are you practising this profession?' It is written, 'Do it *all* in the name of the Lord' (Col. 3:17), and Paul adds, 'I do *everything* to win as many as possible.... Do as I do.'

The separation, or more than that, the divorce that Satan attempts to impose between so-called 'spiritual' and 'socio-lay' activities, cuts our life off from its true dimensions. So we come to that main question:

– What is the *motivation of my life?*

Why do I get up in the morning? Why do I live, work, relax, do projects, get married or stay single? Has God been able to give me a goal for my life, has He been able to make a vertebral column? Have I discovered *my* destiny?

2.5 Denying Ourselves, We Too, Can Win

In reading this chapter, several may realize that even if they are converted, the motivations of their hearts still need to be changed. In this sense, the words of Jesus take on a special significance:

'Then he called the crowd to him along with his disciples and said: "If *anyone* would come after me, he must *deny himself*, and take up his cross and follow me. For whoever wants to save his life will lose it, but whoever loses his life *for me and for the gospel will save it.*"

These phrases are repeated *six times* in the four gospels! It is up to us to recognize what weight God was wanting to put on them! (Matt. 10:39, 16:25, Mark 8:35, Luke 9:24;17:33, John 12:25)

Is it really a matter of us dying? In a sense, yes, but a healthy dying, which, according to these divine words, leads to true life. 'This is what the Lord says – your Redeemer, the Holy One of Israel: I am the Lord your God, who teaches you what is best for you, who directs you in the way you should go. If only you had paid attention to my commands, your peace would have been like a river, your righteousness like the waves of the sea.' (Isa. 48:17-18)

Doubtless there will be some who say, 'Isn't the goal of life to glorify God?' Certainly, but it is impossible to glorify God outside

His will. He is therefore not 'obliged' to be glorified by my hymn-singing, my times of worship, my tithe and my own tailored conception of Christianity, but by a heart who shares the passion of His heart and who gives itself for His cause.

2.6 Giving Yourself in Order to be Given

A young twenty year old from Canada received a call for Upper Volta (now Burkina Faso). His father, a landowner, had prepared a magnificent and secure future for him: farm, cattle, vast, green, Canadian fields. The son was to be the heir of this family estate. When the young man's friends heard about his desire to leave everything for love of Africa, they loudly exhorted him to reconsider his position.

"Think! You don't know anything about those people or their customs. And their language, do you know their language? You won't even be able to make yourself understood! Could you handle the climate? You could get sick and ruin your health! Have you thought of your wife? You'll make her unhappy for sure! And then your children will be uprooted... Think of all the trouble your father has gone to prepare this estate for you; do you want to break his heart?"

Yet this young man made his decision and left his homeland. Every five years, according to the rule, he would go home on furlough and see his old friends again, who were growing older as he was. I had the pleasure of meeting him in a small district of Burkina Faso, and heard his story. He was then sixty. This is what he told our team as we sat around his table.

"Several of my friends have become alcoholics and one of them has committed suicide. All the others, from the ages of twenty until now at sixty, have pursued money and glory. They've told me, 'If only we were twenty years old again, we'd do it all differently.'" And, with a kindly smile that went from ear to ear, this servant of God added, "I have a happy wife, Christian children who are flourishing, hundreds of friends and brothers and sisters in Christ in Burkina Faso. Jesus has been faithful. I am a fulfilled man, and if I had a thousand lives, I would invest them without hesitation for Him and for the Kingdom of God." He added one thing which I shall never forget: "You who are twenty years old now (and he was speaking to committed Christians), consider carefully for whom you want to invest. You have only one life, but with God you can reach the end of it and say, 'If I could start again, I would do the same thing.'"

Charles Marsh, who was a missionary for fifty-two years, mainly in North Africa, expressed the same idea of choice in this way: 'A grain of wheat can be planted or... eaten, but not both.'

In the parable of the four soils, Jesus shows us three ways of existence where the 'seed' lives only for itself and remains sterile; but in the fourth soil, that of the will of God, the seed is multiplied.

Is John 3:16 not the best known verse in the Bible? 'God so *loved* the world that He *gave* His only Son...' To know this verse is to realize that our heavenly Father is always that generous... He still loves the peoples and families of the earth that much. Can He *give* you – as He gave Jesus? So that all those who believe your testimony might not perish but have eternal life?

God only spends what belongs to Him. If He cannot 'spend' you as He wishes, it is because you do not entirely belong to Him.

God is never committed to revealing His will to those who simply want to know what it is for their life, but He will disclose it to those who want to do it (John 7:17).

2.7 To Succeed and Advance is Possible!

Why do so many Christians fail so often in their objectives, though perfectly biblical and inspired by God? Once more it is Paul who gives us the answer when he speaks to Timothy not only of the objectives to reach in order to glorify God, but of the *why*, that is, the *reason*, or again the *motivation*, which he must have if he wants to succeed. Let us read the text carefully:

'Don't let anyone look down on you because you are young, but set an example for the believers in speech, in life, in love, in faith and in purity.' This is already quite a programme, you will agree, but the apostle expects even more from him who would pass on to others the treasure of a life in harmony with the Lord of the universe.

He asks him to apply himself to reading, preaching, teaching and to stirring up the gift which he has already received, to be diligent and to give himself entirely to these things, while watching over himself and his doctrine with perseverance. 'Your *progress*,' he says, 'must be *evident* to everyone.'

Then, in conclusion, Paul gives *the significant reason* for such behaviour: "*Because* if you do [this], you will *save* both yourself and *your hearers*" (1 Tim. 4:12-16).

Blessed were the Christians of the first century! Because they had understood the *why* of all these exhortations, they could put them into practice without finding them painful (1 John 5:3).

God does not have 'little favourites'. He is perfectly just and loyal and we, too, can make visible progress, resembling Jesus more tomorrow than we do today.

The Holy Spirit often sends us 'letters' too; we have plenty of goals and many more unexpressed longings, all holy and desirable, and we wonder why we so often sink into failure or mediocrity. Are we willing today to make the goals *and* motivations of the Lord ours to *want* what He *wants, feel* what He *feels, think* what He *thinks, become sources of blessing for all?* That is the friendship He offers to each of us, but it is a radical choice to make, a *coup d'état* in which I am dethroned in order to make Him King.

Christ does not have two bodies, and if His body, the Church, does not obey, there is no alternative plan or plan of escape. There is a unique work that God has planned for you, which no other person in the entire universe will do. Paul was dethroned to the point of falling to the ground, and he was able to write, 'I no longer live, but Christ lives in me' (Gal. 2:20). His conversion was so radical that for two thousand years, multitudes, probably including each one of us, have benefited from it.

The greatest harvest of all time has begun; the Spirit of God is visiting the continents of the world, and Europe will not be an exception.

The Bible affirms that if the planet Earth is still in existence it is in order that a multitude of people will at last come to Christ through repentance (2 Pet. 3:9-10). Your life, placed on the altar today as a living sacrifice, can become a key in the hand of God. He will multiply it by thirty, sixty or a hundred, and more. By making His passion your passion, you will become His friend.

DETACHABLE PAGE TO RECORD
PERSONAL REFLECTION

Summary of Chapter II, Sharing God's Passion

- God wants all men to be saved (1 Tim. 2:4).
- Jesus came into the world to make this plan possible.
- His return is linked with the proclamation of the Gospel to all people.
- The apostles make it the underlying aim of their ministry.
- The first Christians imitate the apostles.
- We are called, in our work place and our whole life, and with the friends of God in all centuries, to share our Father's passion for the salvation of as many as possible.
- What is the motivation of my life?

My Profession: Am I a 'Christian-mechanic' (replace with your occupation) or a 'mechanic-Christian'? _____

_____

What commitment is the Lord asking of me today in this area of my life? _____

_____

My Motivation: From today, am I ready to do anything for the salvation of as many as possible? Here is my prayer of commitment to God: _____

_____

_____

With this perspective, what are the Holy Spirit's goals that inspire me:

1. In the area of my fellowship with Him: prayer, Bible knowledge, holiness, submission, fruit of the Spirit, spiritual gifts, etc.? _____

_____

2. In the area of my fellowship with Christians? _____

_____

3. Toward non-Christians? (we shall look at several points on this subject in later chapters) _____

_____

4. With respect to my general culture: language, music, etc.?___
_____

5. With respect to my body: healthcare, clothing, habits, sanctification, etc.? _____

_____

'There will be more rejoicing in heaven over one sinner who repents than over ninety-nine righteous persons who do not need to repent.' (Luke 15:7)

Chapter III

Intercontinental Missiles of Blessing

3.1 When it All Began

It was in Geneva in the summer of 1981. In my prayer life, the joy of first love was slowly giving way to an unpleasant sense that I was just turning in ever tighter circles. I had to admit it: my relationship with God was little by little losing its customary savour. To be sure, the daily practice of personal devotions was fulfilling its function as my spiritual motor, but it was running out of steam. Yet that evening, I had the feeling that God had something to say to me, and in spite of being in the throes of an evangelism campaign with four hundred enthusiastic participants, I stayed alone to find out what was in His heart. A well-known text was soon impressed on my mind:

'I urge, then, *first of all*, that requests, prayers, *intercession* and thanksgiving be made *for everyone* – for kings and all those in authority, that we may live peaceful and quiet lives in all godliness and holiness. *This is good, and pleases God* our Saviour, who wants all men to be saved and to come to a knowledge of the truth.' (1 Tim. 2:1-3)

This passage of Scripture was going to turn upside-down not only my fellowship with the Lord, but also my vision of the world and my feelings toward it, and probably set the whole direction of my ministry.

Pray for everyone? Before everything else... First of all? The Holy Spirit seemed to have inspired this text for every Christian to grasp that there is here a priority, an urgency. But how do you put that into practice?

Since then, I have discovered and experimented with several different methods to which I shall refer later, but first the Holy Spirit drew my attention to a book written with the specific goal of furnishing intercessors with information on every country of the world. Entitled *Operation World*, this work provides an overall view of the geographic, political, demographic and spiritual plan for each nation.

Aided by this precious tool, I dedicated twenty minutes each day to praying for a different country. The results were quick in coming! But what were they?

- Amazingly, far from being a boring exercise, those twenty minutes became the best part of my day.
- I began to love countries that I had not even known existed before, and when I heard news about them through the media or, better yet, through meeting one of their citizens, I was truly concerned.
- My prayer life had 'exploded' into one of international dimensions.
- By repercussion, the general quality of my life was renewed and enriched.
- There was a sustained yet natural growth in my general interest in the world, as well as my interest as a missionary.
- Some specific answers to prayer filled me with joy; my fellowship with God was strengthened.
- I left my position as an impotent spectator of history and became an actor in it!
- Even excluding weekends, I found that in one year it was possible to pray for every human being throughout the two hundred and fifty or so nations of the world.

Today, more than ten years later, I am more than ever convinced of the priceless value of this practice, not only for the personal life of every believer, but, even more, for his own country and on to the ends of the earth.

Your room can become a launching pad for intercontinental missiles of blessing!

3.2 An Immense Privilege

Imagine you had a scheme to meet with the head of your country and become his friend. Several months of preparatory steps (even for a brief interview) would still not ensure your success, while, in contrast, it would be very easy for him to meet you, and even to start up a friendship with you. You would doubtless feel highly honoured, and your grandchildren would be sure to hear of it for a long time!

What is it like with God? An audience with Him would be impossible at our own request, and a friendship unimaginable. But the amazing fact is that He Himself has taken the initiative to offer us this audience... and more than that, it is a private, daily meeting! Still more amazing, He actually seeks out our friendship and offers us His (see John 15:15). Are we going to seize this opportunity?

It is easy to confess aloud that He is the King of kings and the Lord of lords, but *our life testifies to or cancels our declaration.*

An audience with the King of the universe, to talk over eternal, dynamic plans, cannot be taken lightly. God is not a religious leader, or a dressed-up king in a parade, like some monarchs these days who have almost no power and are only 'show-pieces' for a nation. It is a fact that God reigns over our political heads and He truly retains *worldly and eternal power.* We cannot take seriously enough the fact that He invites us to enter our own room, close the door and talk with Him about all the men created in His image (Matt. 6:6, John 15:14).

But how could a head of state develop a friendship with someone who refused all conversation concerning the country he was governing and was only interested in talking about himself? Such a relationship would be like that of a father with a very young child, but not like that of two friends!

3.3 A Ministry and a Duty Neither Difficult nor Burdensome

His commands are not burdensome (1 John 5:3); why not? Because, His law being written on our hearts, God causes us to love what He loves (2 Cor. 3:3). How does that happen? His love is poured out into our hearts by the Holy Spirit (Rom. 5:5).

What is the object of His love? God so loved the world... He is the same yesterday, *today* and forever. God still loves the world so much that He asks us, today, before all else, to love it with Him, to become His imitators because we are His beloved children (Eph. 5:1, John 3:16, Heb. 13:8).

I was in Cameroon speaking on this subject to two hundred committed Christians. When I asked the question, "Who knows the passage from 1 Timothy 2:1-3?" almost all of them raised their hands, but when I asked, "Who, since his conversion, has spent ten minutes praying for the Japanese?", only three answered in the affirmative.

They each agreed to take ten minutes the following day to do it. When the time came for the meeting, I wrote upon the board the topic they had received in praying for Japan. One thing was obvious once the board was filled: no Japanese conference, no missionary experience, could have inspired, in so short a time, such precision, such depth and such love for this people. The discreet signature of the Holy Spirit was evident...

3.4 A Unique Opportunity in Eternity

The Earth: A School For Princes (sons and daughters of the King)

A weekly newspaper showed a picture of Prince Charles of Great Britain crawling in the mud, under a barbed wire fence. What a strange posture for such a man! He was in fact training for his pilot's licence.

We are called to reign with Christ for eternity (2 Tim. 2:12). There are myriads of exciting things that we shall be able to do in heaven; imagine for a moment those billions and billions of years of happiness... Of course, worship and fellowship with the brethren will be part of it, which we already experience here to a certain degree, but there are other, very precious things which we can only experience in our few dozen years on this earth, which, in reality, make up only a minute part of our actual life... Here is a very incomplete list of them:

- Loving God without having seen Him.
- Fighting against sin.
- Resisting temptation.
- Interceding for the unbelievers.
- Interceding for the nations.
- Proclaiming the Gospel.
- Leading someone to conversion.
- Forgiving those who have offended us.
- Walking by faith.

Can we grasp how valuable these things are to our God, Who understands the eternal consequences? There is one goal above all that He pursues for every human being: to make us like Jesus Christ (Rom. 8:29). Some accept this plan and others refuse it. Too many Christians imagine that this process will only truly happen once they are in heaven. What devilish deception! What heavy consequences for such an error! Your brief stay on earth is the only place, in the school of the Holy Spirit, where it is possible for you to learn, as

Jesus did, the walk of faith, the fight against sin, faithfulness in opposition, obedience in suffering, love amidst the tears. Have you realized this?

The school for princes is far from being easy, even though there are so many beautiful aspects to it as well: you learn to reign, *you are being prepared*, without fully realizing it, *for your true, eternal, heavenly career.*

What will that be? We do not know. But we do have the certainty that God does everything for one purpose (Prov. 16:4), and He never prepares anything in vain. Eternal life will be much more creative, interesting and beautiful than life on earth. You will be like Jesus Christ, and yet unique in the whole universe, for God's wisdom, goodness and power are infinitely varied. However, we shall not be able to go back, and *our heavenly obedience will never replace our earthly obedience.*

But, you will say, will there be unhappy people in heaven? No. I personally believe that everyone can be perfectly happy in his or her maturity and abilities. An angel will be perfectly happy and will not be jealous of man any more than there will be rivalry between two human beings. Take the example of the present animal kingdom: a horse can be happy as a horse, without envying a trout, a bee or an eagle! Jesus clearly taught us that the way we manage God's gifts on earth will have eternal repercussions (Luke 19:12-26, Rom. 2:6).

Why, at the time of Moses, at the birth of Jesus in Bethlehem, and again today through millions of abortions, does the devil work so hard at destroying babies? One of the reasons is to block off this unique transition period – earthly life – where man can live by faith and glorify God in the face of opposition.

3.5 The Earth: A Planet Loved and Hated

A glorified human body (that of Jesus Christ) is now part of the Trinity (Luke 24:39). Planet Earth is but a tiny grain of dust lost in the immensity of the universe, and yet it was here that God chose to incarnate Himself! Even if innumerable forms of life exist in the cosmos, it is with humans that the Creator of the universe has identified Himself; it is they who receive, by adoption, the title, 'sons and daughters of God', for always.

Yes, our little blue planet is the object of God's attention, and He loves it, even though it has caused Him so much pain. It is upon the earth that the eternal Bride of His Son is being prepared! It is the *obedience* and *prayer* of this Bride that *blesses* the whole earth.

But it is also here upon our world that Lucifer descended in great anger, aiming to steal, slaughter, destroy and spoil creation and, more than that, the creature made in the image of God (John 10:10). From the beginning to the end, he has used and will use *sin* as a springboard to the destruction he intends.

3.6 The Earth: A Village Made to our Measure

From Genesis onwards, the Bible offers an understanding of the universe to every believer. It shows him his collective responsibility, informs him of his origins and the essential stages of his history. To embrace all creation in our dialogue with God is, then, neither new nor superspiritual, but the simple consequence of reading the letter that God addresses to us.

Today, there is greater and more precise information on the world than ever before; the entire planet has been explored, every language recorded, communication is instant and it takes less than twenty-four hours to get from one continent to another. Believers thus have an exceptional opportunity to be interested in, to love, to pray for, all peoples and all situations! More than ever they can identify with their Father in His will and His compassion. Like Him, they can 'adopt' this planet as their own village.

3.7 The Earth: Called to Disappear

'Heaven and earth will pass away, but my words will never pass away." (Matt. 24:35) '...The first earth had passed away.' (Rev. 21:1)

Our earth is decayed, destined to be burned up; is it worth the trouble to take care of it? It is like our own body, which grows old, falls ill, is vulnerable, and returns to the dust. Yet, while it is alive, we are called to take the greatest care of it without making an idol of it, to love it, respect it, preserve it, clothe and nourish it. It is the same for our immediate surroundings and our planet in its entirety. Through our prayer, many vital, even existential, decisions will be inspired by the Spirit of God, and the Destroyer's desire will be frustrated.

In this respect, we can think of all the discoveries made in the fields of ecology, medicine and science; of the national and international decisions on water sciences, cultures, the fight against desert expansion, the discovery of vaccines, etc.. The Christian is not called to adopt a fatalistic attitude, or to rejoice when evil spreads, but, on the contrary, to stand in the gap for the town, country and world in which he lives, and stand to the end.

The Spirit of Christ has inspired our predecessors to a positive and aggressive attitude in the face of ignorance, disease, poverty, deprivation and sin in all its forms. They have researched, invented, improved; they have built universities, hospitals, insurance companies, solidarity movements, and so on. The spirit of fatalism, superstition and fear has held entire nations in a state of bare survival and perpetual oppression.

Jesus went from place to place *doing good* (Acts 10:38). Until His return – and no one knows the date – we must follow in His footsteps. We shall not transform this world into a paradise, but we can bring into it compassion, flavour, light, responses in His name, until the very last day.

3.8 Definite Effectiveness

History is not built on chance, for 'he who prays has his hands on the helm of the world'. This saying is true as far as those hands are inspired by God's Spirit. If only God could convince us that we are not, were never and never will be pawns in His hand, but partners (Rom. 15:16), friends, ambassadors (2 Cor. 5:20). The Lord *does not do anything* without revealing it to His servants, the prophets (Amos 3:7). When a man prays, God listens!

Prayer is a dialogue, a living conversation, not a play where each actor has to content himself with saying his lines. It was much more exciting for God to create someone in His image, capable of love but, therefore, of rebellion, than to create a pawn, seemingly free but secretly manipulated behind the scenes!

Look at how Abraham, Moses, Joshua, Elijah, Hannah, Nehemiah and Ezekiel pray; is it just a 'repeat performance', or the history of humanity struggling in a very real relationship between Creator and creature?

God wanted it this way. He needed neither archangels nor anybody else, but He chose to create sons and daughters who, in spite of His counsel, chose to resist Him, disobey Him and cause Him to weep (Luke 19:41, John 14:9). God's feelings in Genesis 6:5-6 could be translated literally thus: 'His heart was shaken with grief...'. To reign in this way is infinitely more wonderful than pressing buttons.

God did not make man in order to give him an entertaining excursion on the earth, but to save his partner who has gone astray. No, sin is not God's will; no, your obedience is not pre-programmed. Yes, sin shakes God's heart with pain (Gen. 6:6); yes, your obedience causes Him to rejoice (3 John 1:4). Yes, sin really does grieve God and oppose His plans; yes, your prayer really does contribute to the fulfilment of God's will on the earth (Matt. 6:10).

This relationship gives us an indescribably deep sense of our existence; when we take God seriously He also takes us seriously. Each page of the Bible testifies to this, as Hebrews chapter 11 so magnificently reminds us.

God has honoured us by conversing with us over the destiny of peoples and nations, and the repercussions are sure and eternal (Ex. 17:8-13, 32:9-14, Ezek. 22:30).

The press has spoken very little of the one hundred thousand Christians who kneeled in prayer in Timisoara at the dawning of the changes in Romania, of those who interceded for the collapse of the Berlin Wall, and of the people who stood in the gap at the time of the *coup d'état* in Moscow on July 19th, 1991; but the Lord of all the earth sees in secret, takes action and will act again.

> *Ask of me, and I will give you nations as an inheritance, and the ends of the earth as your possession. (Ps. 2:8).*

How do you pray for a nation? What are the areas that most influence its citizens? We see in the history of Israel how much the king's attitude toward God was reflected in the people as a whole. These 'kings' still exist today; they are called the kings of rock music, of tennis, of finance; their power is not only political but crosses all borders, and some have millions of devoted 'fans'. Their reign extends through the media, books, fashion, concerts. Take the case of Mikhail Gorbachev; because of my travelling I can verify that he profoundly influenced a taxi driver in Mali, an ex-communist in France and a minister of culture in Burundi... When Brother Andrew began the project 'Seven Years of Prayer for the USSR' he put a spiritual process into action that extended across the globe!

If we want to see entire nations one day coming to Christ, we must understand what areas shape our society today. Below are seven of the most important of these spheres:

1) *The Church*: its faith, purity, unity, its ministers, its zeal, its growth, faithfulness, etc..

2) *The family*: its need for models, its unity, its future, its tragedies: abortions, lack of care, immorality, divorces, euthanasia, etc..

3) *The government*: the head of state, ministers, governors, administrators, etc.; decisions, management, order and liberty, the fight against organized crime, etc..

4) *Education:* teachers, academic philosophies, universities (nurseries for all tomorrow's leaders), Christian schools, etc..

5) *The sciences, industry, business and finance:* wisdom, research, creativity, Christian presence, etc..

6) *The media:* the philosophy of information, creation and choice of broadcasts, objectivity, journalists (Christian or not), doors open to the Gospel, development of Christian media, etc..

7) *The arts, entertainment and sport:* artists, athletes and their influence on millions of young people, a return to the Creator and Saviour.

3.9 A Choice to Make

For *my house* will be called a *house of prayer* for all nations.

(Isa. 56:7)

We are *his house*...

(Heb. 3:6)

Have you realized that you are the house of God? Today an Old Testament prophecy can become a reality for you, and God could *call you* by a new name: '*House of prayer for all nations.*' That is an original name, is it not? But it is a name that *fits* and *honours you perfectly*, for you are the temple of the Holy Spirit. Is this what you want?

If the apostle Paul were at present passing through your area, and next Sunday he was in your church, above all else he would ask you to pray for all men. Would you do it?

The first Christians had the same nature as we, naturally inclined to unbelief and criticism, preoccupied with their own immediate needs, having their own ideas about 'the people groups that God can't save'. Yet, thousands *did obey* and, because of this, received a *new mentality,* a new way of seeing things. It was in this way that *a very tight international network of prayer* was created, little by little, which worked so well that, when Paul arrived in Italy, this people group was already benefiting from *the faithful intercession of a whole army!*

Throughout the Acts of the Apostles, thousands of people were converted, paralytics were healed, dead were raised, angels intervened, large financial gifts passed from one country to another, missionaries were sent out, towns were turned upside-down by the Gospel. The first Christians seemed invincible, and the Word of God continued to reach new regions... Why? Every new convert, every Christian, every elder, learned, above all else, *to speak to his heavenly Father about all men.* Every Christian learned to love the whole world as God Himself did! Love never dies, it conquers!

Information at that time was, however, very limited; the great majority owned neither book nor map. This should keep us from making information a *sine qua non* for our intercession. Let us use all the information possible to pray better, but let us not forget that it is the Holy Spirit who gives us a true knowledge of needs and the proper way to present them to God (Rom. 8:26).

How can I, at this moment, genuinely and concretely love the Canadians, for example? By allowing them five, ten, or twenty minutes of my 'precious' time, making myself available before the Father and loving them with Him, asking for His blessing and fighting the fight of faith for them.

'I looked for a man among them who would... stand in the gap *before me on behalf of the land so I would not have to destroy it*, but I found none."* (Ezek. 22:30)

Yes, from my own room I can participate in the destiny of Canada, for God not only gives me the opportunity, but expressly asks it of me. The characteristic of the family of which I am a part is a Father who dearly loves a lost humanity. He cares for it, visits it, sends it His messengers, His angels, His missionaries, His prophets, He talks about it in every conversation He has and He happens to have adopted me! When I enter His presence, I sense in His look a passionate love; in His heart, a desire to express Himself; in His thought, a plan of salvation. He says to me, 'Look my son, today I want you to love the Canadians with Me, the Bolivians, the Finns, the people of Gabon, of Thailand...'

I do not understand everything, but I understand enough to work with Him and to make His heart glad.

It is not my will that matters, but His, so I confess my need to be inspired by the Spirit.

Very often, but not necessarily, we begin by praying according to the information we have. Almost imperceptibly inspiration takes over, and God knows how to speak to each of His children. New ideas will develop, that are more profound, bigger, more complete, closer to reality and to the field of prayer; human interest will be replaced by a divine burden; human values will pale as the values of the Kingdom take on greater brilliance; natural love (or the lack of love) will be superseded by the 'so loved' of God. Words will take on a weight until then unknown, our minds will grasp new principles, our whole beings will be concerned and will participate in this spiritual construction process.

When the time is over, it will feel as if we have just had a good conversation with someone; once it is finished, we will say, 'From where did I get such answers, from where did I get that wisdom...?' God is humble; He does not blow a trumpet and announce, 'Attention my son, my daughter, from now on you will be inspired by Me.' No, He does it quietly, almost unnoticeably, but *He does it*. He will do it for you, and for *all those* who want to learn, who want, above all else, to pray for all men.

3.10 What Can I Hope for a Nation?

Listen to how the evangelist Luis Palau responds to this when speaking about his own continent, South America:

> My dream is to see the astonishment of the nations, witnessing the religious revival of a people, who will ask, 'What's happening there?' and who will receive the answer, 'A nation has been converted, and it is God who has done it!'
>
> I hope there will be a general religious revival on this earth as there has been in other times. I believe we are reaching the culminating point of history and that things are going from bad to worse, but that does not mean that we are to give up the fight for the good of the nations. For who can say that the Lord will return three generations from now, or thirty generations?
>
> ... Consider how many millions of people have been converted in the course of the last fifty years! There are

more Christians now than at any other moment in history. I do not think the Bible professes a defeatist philosophy. If that were the case, we would have already given up evangelizing years ago. I expect the return of Jesus Christ in dramatic conditions, like a great cataclysm; but from now until then, I want to work, to hope and to pray for the salvation of thousands, and the improvement of living conditions for the greatest possible number of nations.

I have always been struck with the answer that God gave Abraham when he was interceding for the cities of Sodom and Gomorrah (Gen. 18). Abraham asked God to spare these cities if he found some righteous people there. God agreed to suspend his judgement if the cities sheltered ten of them. For how much greater a reason would the Lord be willing to bless a nation or city! What little number of righteous people does God require in order to suspend his judgement?

I have the conviction that the populations of three countries of Latin America will soon be a majority of evangelicals, professing biblical morals and manifesting love toward our Lord Jesus Christ.

If that happens, I expect God to fulfil what He has promised: the sending of rain, abundant harvests and healing. I truly do not see why such a miracle could not take place.[4]

Who would have believed that Albania (the first atheist country in the world) would now be seeking the Gospel so eagerly, and would see multitudes turning freely to Christ? Who would have foreseen the collapse of communism? The spectacular growth of the Church in China? The intense spiritual thirst throughout black Africa? The conversion of millions in Latin America? The revival in South Korea? The freedom in the Eastern bloc countries? Who but Almighty God...

Hold great hope for your nation, pray according to God's will for the greatest number to come to repentance. Persecution in the midst of revival has been promised us, but whatever different and

---

[4] Translated from Luis Palau, Editions Farel, p. 178.

unexpected forms it may take, it will not be able to stop a multitude of all languages, tribes and peoples calling on the name of Jesus and being saved (Rev. 7:9-10). Persecution sometimes even accelerates the flow of conversions, causes more fervent prayer and purifies the Church!

Jonah was not at all anxious that the city of Nineveh repent, only that his prophecy be realized, as interpreted by his own small personal theology. As for God, He wanted to give the city one last chance to turn from its sin, and so He sent His Word to it.

Are we inspired by the spirit of Jonah, or by the Spirit of God, when we pray for the world? Have we, before the proper time, put a line through this or that nation, refusing it all access to repentance? Let us understand that no philosophy, no movement, no politics, no human belief which raises itself against the knowledge of God, is immortal. Only the Bride of Jesus Christ has the promise of being alive until His return. The nation farthest away from the Gospel, the most sleeping church, can yet be turned around by the breath of God, and benefit from this period of grace. God desires all to come to repentance (2 Pet. 3:9), and what about us? Do we really desire it? Are we greater than He?

'In the last days, God says, I will pour out my Spirit on all people.' (Joel 2:28, Acts 2:17)

''The days are coming,' declares the Sovereign Lord, 'when I will send a famine through the land – not a famine of food or a thirst for water, but a famine of hearing the words of the Lord.'' (Amos 8:11)

3.11 Practical Ideas

A strategy is necessary, and it is up to you to choose what suits you best out of a number of possibilities. Here are a few:

For Your Personal Devotions:

- Pray for *a different nation every day*, or from Monday to Friday, for example.
- Pray for *the same country for one week*, each day covering *one of the seven spheres of influence*.
- Pray for *all the ethnic groups in one nation*, before going on to another.
- Pray for *each nation* with a *specific vision* in mind: that they would humble themselves for their sins / the unreached people groups / revival / heads of state / translation of the Bible, etc..
- Pray for *one continent per month*, for example:

January	–	Africa	April	–	North America
February	–	Europe	May	–	South America
March	–	Asia	June	–	Oceania

- Pray for *your country*: for *every region* or *district,* every *county* or every *parish.* You can set your own pace and length of time spent. French-speaking Switzerland has approximately seven hundred parishes, and... a hundred members of Youth With A Mission. Although we are not setting a schedule, we plan to pray for seven parishes each for three to six months.

Some Sources Of Information:

Books: an encyclopaedia can be an information source, as can a simple geography book in your possession or borrowed from a library.

Small cards: Operation Mobilisation has printed these to aid in intercession for the fifty-two most needy countries.

The media: if Christians made a habit of transforming news into intercession, no major event would take place without being showered with fervent and effectual prayers!

Computer programmes: give a host of information about all nations.

A world map: this is the method I use myself. I have one which is actually a jigsaw puzzle, which I have hung on the wall of my office. Each day, after hearing the news and listening to the Lord for the subject of His choice, I intercede for a particular country. By sticking a pin in between the puzzle pieces, I indicate the nation for which I have prayed, until all have been covered.

If, perhaps, you are teaching this subject to others and you have none of these items available, encourage them to make a list of countries about which they know and begin with them. God will be faithful to provide when we obey Him.

Maps of the continents, taken from the YWAM International Prayer Agenda, have been added to this book to help those who do not have other sources of information. If this is the case with you, you could colour in or underline countries in the way that would be most helpful for you with the strategy you have chosen.

For Your Prayer Group:

If you meet weekly, why not decide to devote one meeting per month to one country? You can begin with the country you like best, or one where those in the group may know friends, missionaries, or one with crying needs. It would be good to decide on a specific basic strategy; for example, for as many months as the group meets, each person will present a country of his own choice for prayer. This presentation can be done in whatever way is preferred by the individual, as long as prayer is kept as the priority rather than the report itself. Especially for the first few times, the most motivated should take up the responsibility, so that the preparation as well as the application is seen as a celebration rather than a work duty!

For many, this will seem like entering an unexplored cave; no one knows where it will lead, or what wonders are hidden within it. Your group may begin very timidly, yet little by little become a real spiritual pillar for a missionary family, a city or a whole people group. This could in turn lead to correspondence with someone from the country in question, and, who knows, maybe a visit to that country. Perhaps a member of your group will even become the answer to your prayers and be called to that nation. If your group sows love, it will reap life, abundant life for those who put themselves aside to give and serve the Kingdom of God.

For Concerts of Prayer:

Be creative: the people of God can be very effective as long as the leader's trumpet call is clear! To set up a concert of prayer is to gather an army; prepare meticulously for the combat, and you will read the victory on their faces. People come, and come back again, to what they like and where they feel useful. A leader mainly has four elements to manage:

1. *Information on the subject or subjects of prayer*: it must be interesting, brief, precise and stimulating.

2. *Different aspects of activity*: songs (expressing a message of faith, combat, gratitude in relation to the subject being dealt with), times of silence, prophetic utterance, prayer (in all its forms), proclamation out loud, etc..

3. *Groups of intercessors*: if you have one hundred and fifty people, you can lead them in prayer at different times by cell groups of two, five, ten, or even twenty people. Sometimes they can be divided in just two groups, one interceding while the other proclaims the victory of Christ in song. Sometimes the subject will be the same for everyone, at other times each group will take on a different aspect, for example, ten groups each praying for the ten districts of a city or the ten regions of a country, and so forth.

4. *Times of prayer*: these should be long enough for some worthwhile and varied activity, for example, ten minutes of intercession for the international conference of x, five minutes for the president of y. If people pray in groups of limited size, the majority will be able to say something.

At the time of the worldwide week of prayer, I had to lead five hundred people for ten minutes. I took up the idea of praying for all men. In order to do this, I photocopied a list of all the countries and cut it into as many pieces. Baskets containing the tiny papers were passed along the rows, and every second person took a paper and prayed with his neighbour. What a joy to think that in one single place, more than two hundred pairs of disciples were praying for the whole world. This was one of the high points of the week.

Summary of chapter III, Intercontinental Missiles Of Blessing

My house will be called: House of prayer for all nations

(Isa. 56:7)

- In secret in my own room, I can love and influence the whole world.
- My privilege: to talk with the Head of the universe! To be His friend.
- A ministry and a duty, neither difficult nor burdensome: the Holy Spirit inspires, motivates and nourishes my prayer.
- A unique opportunity in eternity: I live in a school for princes, on a planet loved and hated; it is my 'village' but it will one day disappear. My responsibility is real.
- Seven spheres which shape our society and require prayer:
  - ✝ *The Church*   ✝ *Education*
  - ✝ *The family*   ✝ *The arts*
  - ✝ *The government* ✝ *The media*
  - ✝ *The sciences*
- The choice to pray for all men, in my personal devotions and with others, belongs to me.

When am I going to begin to intercede for the nations? _____

What will be my first strategy?

_____

Testimony of my first answers to prayer:

1. _____
2. _____
3. _____

How and when am I going to have my prayer group start on intercession for the nations (why not read this chapter together)?

_____

How can my church be trained in prayer for the nations?

_____

How can I organize or inspire a concert of prayer in my city or region? _____

_____

Chapter IV

Missiles for the Salvation of Others

Is there a connection between prayer for someone and his salvation?

The passage we studied in the preceding chapter also gives an answer to this vital question. Let us look at it again:

'I urge, then, first of all, that requests, prayers... be made *for everyone....* This *is good,* and *pleases God* our Saviour, who wants *all men to be saved* and to come to a knowledge of the truth' (1 Tim. 2:1-4).

As is his habit, Paul practises what he teaches: 'Brothers, my heart's desire and *prayer to God for the Israelites* is that *they may be saved"* (Rom. 10:1).

The New Testament, then, answers an unequivocal *yes* to the question. The first Christians received this teaching from the moment of their conversion and its being put into practice was like the coal in the steam engine of the propagation of the Gospel!

In a time of revival in the nineteenth century, certain notorious sinners heard that the Christians had begun to pray for their salvation. In the following days, in spite of their mistrust, very few resisted the conviction of the Holy Spirit that seized them!

More recently, during the Vietnam war, a chaplain gathered the soldiers he had led to Christ. Together they decided to pray, with fervour and unity, for the salvation of their wives back in the United States. A few weeks later, several of them received letters that read something like this:

> *Dear, something incredible has just happened in my life. I was working in the kitchen one morning as usual, when all of a sudden I saw my life just as if God Himself was showing it to me... I realized that I have lived selfishly, ignoring His existence. I felt so dirty and guilty, but then I realized that He wanted to forgive me and take my life into His hands. I gave my life to Christ and it's wonderful. I*

don't know how you'll take this... Just know that I love you more than ever.

These examples thrilled me personally, but they also pose an important question: is salvation irresistible? Did these people still have the freedom to refuse it?

Let us take the example of your favourite meal. If you could choose between that and some nauseating scrap of food, which would you choose? Those wives simply had the immense privilege of benefiting from the intercession of a fervent team. They were in no way forced to come to conversion (and it is sadly probable that not all of them did), but they understood the truth of their real condition without Christ. For the first time in their lives, the filth of sin was no longer being compared with the spirit of this age, but was put under the floodlights of the holiness of God!

In fact:

– The veil which was preventing them from seeing the light of the glory of the Gospel and feeling the unconditional love of God, was torn apart. (2 Cor. 4:4)

– The 'anti-Christ' reasonings that they had entertained were exposed and defeated in the spiritual realm. (2 Cor. 1 0:4-5)

– The angels, who are spirits sent to serve those who will inherit salvation, were put into action at the command of Him who called them: God Himself! (Heb. 1 :14)

It is still true, as it was with some of the inhabitants of Jerusalem for whom Jesus wept in His time, that there are people today who shut themselves up in their pride and wickedness when faced with the open arms of Christ. But there are others, in fact multitudes, who receive and who will receive the love of God with immense gratitude when it is revealed to them.

The contemporary world has given birth to a mentality so individualistic that we have trouble understanding the laws concerning the impact our sin, or our obedience, can have on a third party, a group, or a whole society. It is true that each individual will render an account for his own life and his acceptance or refusal of grace. But God also judges cities and nations, for sin as well as holiness, while not forced on others, is 'contagious'.

'Through the blessing of the upright a city is exalted, but by the mouth of the wicked it is destroyed.' (Prov. 11:11)

'Righteousness exalts a nation, but sin is a disgrace to any people.' (Prov. 14:34)

From a negative point of view, it is easy to understand these influences when we read such newspaper headlines as this: 'TWO-YEAR-OLD GIRL IS MOWN DOWN BY A DRUNKEN DRIVER WHO LOSES CONTROL OF HIS CAR...' The negative example that is most difficult to admit is the entrance of sin into the world through our first parents, Adam and Eve.

But what of the positive influence? Would God make spiritual laws that work only one way? Of course not! We always mention the sin that is punished to the third and fourth generations, but we forget the blessing that lasts for *a thousand generations*! (Deut 5:10).

Every human being, therefore, has the immense privilege as well as the awesome responsibility of having an influence not only on his contemporaries (space), but also in history! When a man begins to love and fear God, the chain of the curse is broken, and is replaced by a blessing that can last thousands of years!

Is not God wonderful? In His impartiality, He yet reserves the right to be generous when His children pray! His grace is not kept for those who deserve it, but for those who ask for it.

'In accordance with your great love, forgive the sin of your people.... The Lord replied, 'I have forgiven them, as you asked.' (Num. 14:19-20)

Through His creation, the discernment of good and evil, and awareness of eternity, God has given a testimony of Himself to all men.

Through the work of Christ, reconciling His love and His justice, He offers forgiveness to all (Rom. 11:32). Today, He chooses to take account of the intercession of His people to bring light to those who walk in darkness.

In this chapter we are going to study six biblical principles which can enrich and inspire our hidden life of intercession for the unconverted.

4.1 Nothing is Impossible to God

An English Christian had been praying for nine months for the conversion of his neighbour without seeing the slightest sign of change. Then God showed him the reason: he simply did not believe that this man could be converted! Humbly he recognized the fact, but what could he do?

"What can you believe?" asked the Lord.

Upon reflection, he realized he had never addressed one single word to his neighbour, so in the following week he prayed that God would open up a conversation between them. He could believe for that much...

A few days later, while he was working in the garden, his neighbour came out to do the same thing – and a conversation started very naturally over the hedge.

This little encouragement inspired our friend to apply the same principle for the following week: for what can I actually believe? In prayer, he asked for the privilege of doing some service for his neighbour.

On the Wednesday his doorbell rang.

"My lawnmower has broken down; could I borrow yours?"

The Christian could have leapt and danced for joy! But, with perfect self-control, he contented himself with lending his lawnmower...

The third week, he told himself that what was happening had to be more than chance, and steeled himself to pray for a new 'faith push': "Lord, I want my neighbour to come to my home for tea." No sooner said than done – for the first time, his neighbour crossed his threshold!

The fourth 'faith push' was crucial: "Lord, let me speak to him about you in the course of the week." The two men soon found themselves out in their gardens...

"What do you all do together on Sunday mornings?" enquired the neighbour. "I always see your family pack into the car..."

From there it was not difficult to talk about the church service, and an interesting conversation followed.

The fifth week, the Christian prayed, then invited his neighbour to come with him to a Christian meeting.

The sixth week, he prayed for the man to pass from darkness into the light, from the kingdom of Satan to the kingdom of God... and his neighbour came to Jesus Christ!

This authentic story underlines a truth as simple as it is important: God is committed to responding to our faith (not to our unbelief)!

An evangelist once asked his audience, "How do you swallow an elephant?" Everyone knew the thing was impossible... until the answer came, "You just have to cut it into little pieces!"

You have been praying, perhaps for years, for the conversion of a family member or a friend, but you really feel as if you are trying to 'lift an elephant'.

In fact, are you secretly thinking. 'He (or she) will never be converted, anyway!'? If this is so, start again today with a 'faith push' for which you can truly believe, and the elephant will begin to get smaller...

Take the example of a particularly difficult case, and let Jesus speak to us:

'"How hard it is for the rich to enter the kingdom of God! Indeed, it is easier for a camel to go through the eye of a needle than for a rich man to enter the kingdom of God." Those who heard this asked, *"Who then can be saved?"* Jesus replied, "What is impossible with men *is possible with God."'* (Luke 18:24-27)

4.2 Demolishing Arguments...

Our weapons of war are not just human. They draw their power from God, who renders them capable of destroying the strongholds in which men have barricaded themselves against Him. Yes, we demolish arguments and sophisticated pretensions that set themselves up against the true knowledge of God. Taking every rebellious thought captive, we bring it to obedience to Christ and to recognition of His authority (2 Cor. 10:4-5).

The Spirit of God searches everything, knows everything. He knows the arguments that have set themselves up in the unconverted person, keeping him far from Christ. It is your privilege as intercessor to receive the mind of the Lord on this subject, as He says Himself, 'I no longer call you servants, because a servant does not know his master's business. Instead, I have called you friends, for everything that I learned from my Father I have made known to you' (John 15:15).

The ferment of these arguments can be pride, religiosity, unbelief, hardness, incomprehension, distrust, individualism... but also things that appear to be more noble, like reputation, this or that education, culture or philosophy. For myself it was timidity that forbade the fourteen-year-old teenager that I was to attend Christian meetings which I heard about.

Happily, several people were already praying for me, and shortly afterwards I discovered for myself the abundant life in Christ.

Even for someone very close to us, we do not naturally know what the right thing to ask in our prayers is (cf. Rom. 8:26). If we do not allow the breath of God to inspire our words, we shall quickly fall into vain repetitions which Jesus identifies with pagan practices (Matt. 6:7). It is precisely for this reason that the Holy Spirit wants to be our 'teacher'. He is going to accomplish with us and through us, with a view to our neighbour's conversion, *an ordered and progressive work of spiritual liberation*.

How do we proceed?

- Express to the Lord your availability as an intercessor for this or that person.

- Remain silent, and wait in faith for a first thought for the person in question; we shall call him Bob, as an example.

- Pray, plead, intercede before God in accordance with the thought you had, until it has been completely covered.

- If the Spirit reveals a 'rebellious' argument in that person, you could express yourself thus: 'I resist in faith and in the name of Jesus, who has received all power in heaven and on earth, this argument of unbelief which is preventing Bob from seeing his true condition before God...'

- Your prayer could have several extensions, for God will lead you to 'water' every aspect of Bob's life where unbelief needs to be uprooted and where faith can be sown: what he *reads*, his *work situation*, his *friendships* and *contacts*, his *dreams*, his *memories*, his *concerns*, his *failures* and *successes*, his *frustrations*, his *goals*, and still many *other facets*.

- You can also pray in this way with two, three or more others. Why not try it during a break at work or in class? Fifteen minutes of specific intercession in the presence of God can be more effective than years of wandering prayers.

4.3 Use Your Legal Right

On a visit to the bank, your attitude will differ completely depending on whether you are going to withdraw your money, or to try to get a job as a secretary. In the first situation, you will politely but firmly claim what belongs to you. In the second, you will be asking a favour; you will therefore be on your best behaviour and making the most of your good qualities, especially if you have been unemployed for six months and twenty other applicants have come before you, hoping for the same position!

The righteous are as bold as a lion, Proverbs tells us (28:1). We are righteous because Christ has become the 'Lamb of God' who takes away the sin of the world. He has justified us and purified us.. Do you believe He has done a good work? Of course! It is the greatest masterpiece in the whole history of humanity, the only reason why you and I can be full of assurance. But what I want to underline here, is that our prayer for salvation is also a perfectly just prayer! God knows it, and so does Satan, as well as the angels and demons.

The passing of someone from the kingdom of darkness to the Kingdom of God will be greatly encouraged with the benefit of the prayer of a righteous person, and all the more so if the righteous one intercedes as someone conscious of his rights and not as a beggar.

Jesus is doubly worthy of receiving eternal worship from the unconverted person for whom you pray. It is He who *created* him and He who *redeemed* him. For the person, each day that passes and that should have been used to glorify God, is a day that Satan steals through rebellion and sin. In passing, let me emphasize that this is also why no one can misuse the patience of God by saying, 'Wait, I just want to live three more weeks in sin and then I'll get converted!'

Let us look closely at the passages which serve as the basis for our authority in this area:

'*You are worthy*, our Lord and God, to receive glory and honour and power, for you *created* all things, and by your will they were created and *have their being*.' (Rev. 4:11)

'Then I looked and heard the voice of many angels, numbering thousands upon thousands, and ten thousand times ten thousand. They encircled the throne and the living creatures and the elders. In a loud voice they sang: "Worthy is the Lamb, who was slain, to receive power and wealth and wisdom and strength and honour and glory and praise!"

'Then I heard *every creature in heaven and on earth and under the earth* and on the sea, and *all that is in them,* singing: "To him who sits on the throne and to the Lamb be praise and honour and glory and power, for ever and ever!"' (Rev. 5:11-13)

Is it not amazing that even those 'under the earth' will recognize God's perfect justice? Not a single creature in the entire universe, lost or saved, will dispute the righteousness of God and the fact that He is indeed worthy to receive all glory. Would it not be better for man to recognize this now, and to profit from the consequences for and during his life on earth?

How much more should we, who have received the grace to understand these things, make use of the powerful weapon of prayer, that the Lamb would receive the praise of those whom we long to claim from the thief!

When one human being prays for the salvation of another human being, the devil and his lies draw back and the angels get to work!

4.4 A Fervent Prayer

In 1977, I was living in M'Pouto, a little village in the Ivory Coast, a few kilometres from Abidjan. At that time, this pioneer YWAM base was the only one in the whole of West Africa, and we were a team of only six in all. The work was varied: housework, gardening, plumbing and a few 'spiritual' activities, but I terribly missed doing evangelism.

One Monday morning, I cried out to the Lord, telling Him of my desire to serve faithfully and humbly in all the material obligations, but asking fervently that He grant me the privilege of leading one person to Christ in the course of the week.

A little later, while we were at the airport to meet a visitor, a child of nine or ten began to harass me in the arrival hall, wanting to polish my shoes. I had neither the means nor the intention of letting him do so, but he would not listen and, armed with his cleaning gear, he stuck to me like a shadow. Finally, remembering my prayer, I wondered if this child was not in fact sent to me by God. One short conversation confirmed it: he was more than willing to commit his life to Christ! So it was in the air-conditioning and comfortable chairs of the Abidjan airport that God used me to witness the decision of this young boy.

The following Monday I offered the same prayer. No evangelism had been planned, but my desire to lead someone to Christ surpassed everything. I did not ask for health, or finances, or anything else, concentrating entirely on the main objective, the salvation of a human being...

On the Tuesday, an unknown visitor of about twenty years of age appeared at our door. According to the local custom, he came simply to greet us. I 'greeted' him back by presenting him with the salvation of Jesus Christ. He received him personally after the third visit in that same week.

The next week, an alcoholic in the village had a dream, and came spontaneously to us to get his life in order with God. The fourth week, his wife, kneeling beside her husband, in turn gave her life to Christ.

One of the great lessons of my fifteen-month stay there came from those four weeks when God emphasized for me one of His eternal promises: 'The *fervent* prayer of a righteous man accomplisheth much" (Jas. 5:16, KJV).

Jesus sometimes prayed with great cries and tears (Heb. 5:7). If a child is in danger of death, I cannot speak to his parents lightly, or just in passing; the gravity of the situation requires my greatest attention. In the same way, when I am speaking of a person's eternal salvation and his relationship with his Creator and Saviour, fervency of heart is only normal.

4.5 Daring Prayer

There was once a grandmother who lived opposite a school full of young people, and God put it in her heart to pray for the salvation of one student. So she persevered in that prayer, also adding, "Lord, I pray that thousands of others will be saved through this young man…"

Some time later, George Werver was converted at the age of eighteen and became the founder of Operation Mobilisation!

Before the Olympic Games in Los Angeles in 1984, groups of women undertook to pray by name for every street of this metropolis of almost a hundred kilometres' diameter. During the Games, some eleven thousand Christians from all over the world were received by eight hundred local churches for a huge evangelistic outreach.

Almost one thousand people a day made a profession of faith. Athletes from every continent and many closed countries heard the Good News. Carl Lewis, a quadruple gold medallist and 'king' of the Games, gave his testimony as a committed Christian in a newspaper which was distributed in bulk at the doors of the stadium!

But the most astonishing testimony came from a chief of police, informing us that not one violent death had been reported during the fifteen days of the Games. Normally, the daily count averaged at forty-eight throughout the year! During this period, Los Angeles became a secure city, although criminals of every type could have taken advantage of the opportunity represented by the three million extra visitors…

In response to the daring prayer of Christians, God had sent His heavenly armies into the streets of the 'city of angels' and His Kingdom grew, while the gates of Hell drew back.

When I was born my four grandparents had already died, but through marriage I inherited a fervent and daring grandmother. Her parents had been assassinated in the Armenian tragedy and, at the age of eleven, she became a slave to the Turks in her own home. Converted to Christ, she finally reached France and joined the Salvation Army. From then on, she did not cease to pray for her husband and her whole family.

Today, five of her seven children are in key positions in the Lord's service, as are a large number of her grandchildren. Like Joseph in his time, she grasped the fact that daring prayer can change distress and deportation into salvation for an entire family, and for thousands of others.

The greatest and most beautiful gift you could give to a non-Christian is to intercede for his salvation.

4.6 Obedient Prayer

This chapter would be incomplete if it did not mention the fact that the Holy Spirit almost always leads the intercessor into some practical steps. The love that God pours out into our hearts is never sterile; it engenders, in prayer, an abundance of creative ideas.

We were preparing an evangelism campaign for a city of four thousand five hundred inhabitants in the French part of Switzerland. In prayer, the Lord clearly showed us that we were not to content ourselves with some four hundred people coming to the meetings, but to think in terms of the four thousand one hundred others. He inspired in us a strategy of twelve points, which gave us an entirely different perspective on evangelism and on His love for all.

1. Division of the city into twenty-two sections, which were then completely canvassed. Out of one thousand one hundred families, six hundred accepted an excellent tract and two hundred received us into their home.
2. Meeting with the aged.
3. Meeting with those studying the catechism.
4. Meeting with pupils in religion classes.
5. Film and activities for children and teenagers.
6. Child evangelism in the afternoons.
7. A team visiting every restaurant and bar.

8. Newspaper articles.
9. Broadcasts over the local radio station.
10. Open air meetings.
11. Street contacts and literature distribution.
12. Evening meetings for everybody.

Let us hold on to the principle: prayer without obedience is sterile, but obedient prayer is the source of salvation and life. The apostle James emphasizes this magnificent truth and resumes it here:

'As the body without the spirit is dead, so faith without deeds is dead.' (cf. Jas. 2:14-26)

Prayer and evangelism are the two oars of your personal ministry. He who only prays will end up turning his boat in circles, and so will he who evangelizes without praying (more rare). What is even better, if your youth group or prayer group sets itself to pray in concert, your progress could look like a rowing competition!

The next chapter introduces us to various practical possibilities.

DETACHABLE PAGE TO RECORD
PERSONAL REFLECTION

Summary of Chapter IV, Missiles for the Salvation of Others

The Bible establishes a direct link between prayer and salvation. When a human being prays for the salvation of another human being, the devil and his lies draw back and the angels of God get to work!

The keys for an effective prayer:

- Nothing is impossible to God; make 'faith pushes'.
- Demolish anti-Christ arguments.
- Use your 'legal' right.
- Have fervent prayer.
- Have daring prayer.
- Have obedient prayer.

Who are the non-Christians for whom the Holy Spirit asks me to pray faithfully?

1. _____
2. _____
3. _____

What moment in the week shall I dedicate to this?

_____

What are the 'faith pushes' I am making progress in?

Name:_____

Subjects:_____   Fulfillment:_____

_____   _____

_____   _____

___   ___

Name:_____

Subjects:_____   Fulfillment:_____

_____   _____

_____   _____

___   ___

Name:_____

Subjects:_____   Fulfillment:_____

_____   _____

_____   _____

___   ___

If I know the people who prayed for my own conversion, how can I express my gratitude to them? _____

_____

_____

Chapter V

Using Your Talents for the Harvest: Adaptable Methods

The wisdom of God is infinitely varied; in fact, if we were to find something constant in the ways of the Holy Spirit, it would surely be innovation and creativity!

Many Christians today desire fervently to be witnesses, and deep in their hearts they long to bear much fruit; yet, just as the size of a shoe can be wrong, so the three or four methods of evangelism of which they know do not seem really to fit them.

This chapter will therefore be a collection of practical and applicable ideas which have been tried and tested. Many readers may find the shoe that fits their foot, while others will doubtless discover clues to help them find something their 'size'... So, let's go!

5.1 Hospitality

How many Christians have you invited to dinner in the past year? And how many non-Christians? These latter will completely disappear from our areas of concern if we do not make a deliberate effort to establish or keep contact with them. We have confused separation from sin with separation from sinners. Jesus exhorts us to separate ourselves from the corrupt system of the world, but He never asked us to detach ourselves socially and culturally from society. On the contrary, He teaches us by His own example to be the friend of sinners, to eat with them (Matt. 11:19), to invite in those who cannot do the same for us. Would the Pharisees have convinced us that it is a sign of spirituality to associate only with people like us?

If there is a situation to put right, it is in this area. Let us begin at the beginning. I challenge you with the same challenge I am endeavouring to take up again myself: *at least once a month, to invite some non-Christians to dinner.*

Here are a few occasions not to miss as opportunities to invite your neighbours over:

- Your arrival in a new neighbourhood.
- The birth of a child.
- The inauguration of something.

An invitation for a drink is a good method. Use the opportunity to offer a small gift as your guests leave: a book, cassette, etc..

A Slide Evening

A trip, vacation, a Christian camp, a topical slide show... your boxes of slides may hide unsuspected treasures! While many of our contemporaries would not come to an evangelistic meeting, they would willingly come to your home for a slide show. Such an evening can help develop a friendship, get through to a couple in a warm and peaceful family setting, act as a catalyst for a significant conversation, build trust in your neighbours for the children's club, break the ice and the distrust in your apartment block... and above all, serve as pre-evangelism!

A missionary friend had the idea of very naturally including a slide depicting a blind man who was healed, mentioning it in the same tone of voice as when he was explaining what a loquat or a baobab tree is, without any special emphasis. At a break for coffee, someone asked him, "What did you mean about the blind man who was healed?"

That can happen in your home, too!

A Video Evening

This is the same principle as with the slides, except that it is possible to give a more complete, professional and focussed testimony. There are more and more films and themes to which no one can remain indifferent. If you own a video system, why not dedicate it to the Lord and organize 'evangelism' evenings? Sometimes we spend a lot of money to get three non-Christians into a church; that is good and it should be done, but let us take hold of the vision, as a church if necessary, of regularly gathering non-Christians into our homes.

Your ministry will be that of an ambassador: to know the videos that present your heavenly kingdom, to know the needs of the people around you, and to offer your living room as a meeting place.

5.2 Correspondence

This is a hidden and little recognized ministry, but it deeply touches people's hearts. Maybe you often hear such remarks as, 'The note you sent me was exactly what I needed.' If that is the case, God is certainly going to inspire you with a lot more letters. Maintain regular correspondence with non-Christian friends; remember their birthdays; pray for new correspondents: the lonely, the sick, prisoners, childhood friends, distant relatives.

The Answering Machine

A pastor in France had about fifty people at his services. Thanks to an answering machine and a few well-placed announcements, his telephone congregation was as large as eight hundred and twenty in one week!

You may be shy, yet feel that God often gives you a burden for those near you. Would you be willing, then, to walk around with a microphone sometime and record a few testimonies to play on your answering machine? This does require an investment in order to begin, but if the Lord is calling you, He will bless your small beginnings.

The Telephone, Fax, Electronic Mail

One woman telephones seven people each day, following the numbers in the local directory. It is a very specific ministry which the 'Jesus people' used a great deal in the 70s in the United States. Too often we tend to believe that the person contacted in this manner will be disturbed and annoyed by the call, forgetting the one who would be happy finally to discover someone ready to listen and sincerely interested in his life.

These means of communication have been very successful, and the media uses them freely, as, because of their anonymity, people tend to open up more readily.

The operation 'New Life for All' in Basel, Switzerland, began its campaign with forty thousand telephone calls to offer a tract. One year later, one hundred and fifty Bible study groups averaged six new people per group, that is, nine hundred people who had come, or come back, to Christ by this means!

Bible Calendars

One good message is fine; three hundred and sixty-five is better...
This is a ministry requiring perseverance. The first year you will
give away perhaps a dozen calendars, and not all of them will be
read. But your perseverance will be rewarded when, year after year
at Christmas time, dozens, if not hundreds of families, will be
expecting your visit.

One of the advantages of the calendar is that it is available in a
large number of languages; if you live in an area with a lot of
immigrants, think about it!

Bibles, Gospels, Literature

Even if this is a work of sowing rather than reaping, it is the
leaven which has turned around entire people groups and will
continue to do so.

In Africa, many unemployed Christians could earn their living as
Bible salesmen. I remember visiting all the administrative offices of a
small town in Mali and selling thirty Bibles in a single morning.

In the West, many have a Bible somewhere, in the attic or on the
bookshelf, but have in fact only a vague idea what it really is.
Sowing a city with a well-presented Gospel will revive in many a
desire to read more of it and know more about it.

In Longwy (in north-west France), a team from Operation
Mobilisation covered the whole town with a brochure offering a Bible
course. Sometime later, the forty people who asked for the course
were visited by YWAM; in two weeks, four of them had given their
lives to Christ, two of whom were teenagers and one a grandmother
in her nineties!

Some Christians edit a letter or small newspaper for their
neighbourhood; it is original, personalized, and when you organize a
trip to the mountains, a women's meeting or a table tennis
competition, your neighbours turn up...

Book Stands, Cassettes, CDs

More than thirty thousand people have been born again in France
through this means. In 1950, a pastor had a Bible stand at the market
in Lisieux. An illiterate woman came by and accepted a tract, which
she stuffed in the bottom of her bag. Some time later, her son fell
gravely ill, and she remembered that the pastor had talked to her
about prayer for the sick. She searched out the crumpled-up paper

and found the pastor's address on it. He prayed for the child, who was miraculously and totally healed.

This event served as the detonator for a revival among the gypsies which still continues today, and the conversion to Jesus Christ of more than thirty thousand of them!

Once when I told this story in a church in the south of France, a man came up to me.

"Do you know," he said, "that the pastor of whom you spoke... was me!" He simply confirmed that things had indeed happened that way.

It is often a thankless task to persevere through thick and thin and to hear nothing but a faint echo from the population. The Lord had not said to this pastor, 'Listen, a woman will come, you will speak to her about my compassion for the sick and give her a tract, and through this I shall save more than thirty thousand people.' No, this man had continued as usual, and sown in hope...

Newspaper Articles

Newspapers are not like advertisements; people pay for them, and so they read them!

Here are three possibilities:

a) Letters from readers: as we are salt and light, your opinion is important. Abortion, war, indifference, sects, temptations, drugs, faithfulness, courage, trust, faith, are some of the themes about which the Holy Spirit would like to speak in our newspapers and cannot, for want of prophets.

b) Regular or one-time articles which you can compose or gather voluntarily for your newspaper. If you take a trip, hold a social activity with your youth group, or have a march for Jesus, write an article about it. Once I was given a whole page to report on a missionary trip, photos included! Recently, a newspaper with a circulation of a hundred and twenty thousand accepted for publication a letter entitled 'Deserving or celebrating your birthday'. Ask, do not throw in the towel before trying! Pray, then, equipped with a thought-through and attractive proposition, knock at the right door!

c) You have just read a particularly powerful or striking testimony and you think, if only those around me could know about this! Then you calculate how much it would cost to reproduce the page one hundred thousand times, and the time it would take to slip it into as many letter-boxes.

A quicker, cheaper method is to have your article published in a newspaper that has a large circulation. Of course, that will also cost an appreciable sum, but what a beautiful gift for a hundred thousand families... Oh, I forgot... when was the last time you addressed a hundred thousand people or families?

Local Radio

I have a childhood friend who would probably not be at ease if he was asked to stop people in the street and tell them Jesus loves them. However, the moment a local radio station was begun, he had it in his heart to collaborate with them. His broadcast, titled, 'Joy of Living', has gained third place on the chart of the listeners' favourite transmissions. It runs for thirty minutes every fortnight, and thus reaches people by the thousand. Dozens of interviews have enabled the public to discover the riches of the Christian world. And since for many people, the extent of Christian music was a few old hymns, they were astonished to hear, broadcast after broadcast, an almost inexhaustible repertoire.

How many Christians, in Switzerland or elsewhere, have the chance to testify of their faith regularly, to several thousand people? Not many... Why not participate yourself? Local radio broadcasts are a means of penetrating every home in your city or village; all you need is a clear, striking message, a good cassette recorder, some creative ideas and... all the best to you!

Book, Cassette, Video Libraries

This idea consists in making freely available to everybody, subjects as contemporary and interesting as possible, for example, (biblical) sexuality, genetic manipulation, New Age, integration, the next world, ecology, etc..

You can begin at a modest level, particularly concentrating your efforts on your colleagues, friends and relatives. It can also be pictured on a large scale, the operation being supported by your church and preceded by advertising.

A church in Lausanne records every service on video. Many of our contemporaries would not refuse seeing something of your life 'to get an idea', especially if it is in private, in front of their own television set, and the church service is well chosen!

Children's Clubs

These can be started in a family, on the occasion of a birthday, for example. Or you could begin in the open air, with help at the beginning from one or two experienced people whom you would choose carefully. Or again, you could put a notice in the stairwell of the neighbouring apartment blocks, saying something like: 'Local news: children's club (Christian orientation) for 5 to 7 year olds, Wednesdays at 2 to 4 p.m.. If interested, contact Mrs Brown before Sept. 30th, building F, tel. 65-893632.'

Crèche, Babysitting

The world is set up in such a way that if we respond to someone's immediate need, he will reveal his deep need.

How many couples would love to spend a romantic evening together, but a babysitter costs too much, and they do not know anyone they can really trust? How many mothers long for a free morning from time to time! Giving up one or two mornings a month to serve the neighbouring women would give you the opportunity to make new acquaintances and friends among them.

Visiting The Sick At Home Or In Hospital

The pastor Juan Carlos Ortiz was looking for help to practise this ministry. He felt that one of his parishioners would make a good visitor, but she was very reticent. One day he called her to his office, and to help overcome her fears, he explained to her in minutest detail what she would need to do: 'Take this bus and get off at this stop... Ring the bell and say this... At the sick person's bedside, read this passage of Scripture... Pray like this and say...' The woman finally agreed. Late that night the pastor had a very excited voice on the line: she had applied his explanations to the letter, and not only had things gone well, but the sick person was healed! Needless to say, nothing can stop this parishioner today, in her zeal for this new ministry.

In the eyes of my father, all Europeans were Christians, until the day he got cancer and was hospitalized sixty kilometres from his friends and acquaintances. He received two types of visit, both kind, no doubt, but he longed for Bible reading, and spontaneous prayer did him good. Some visitors prayed and read the Bible, others did not. This difference, of little importance to him in the past, became singularly significant now that he was at the doors of eternity.

Throughout his whole life he had spoken of 'the good God', but before passing away, he was speaking about Jesus, who was coming to take him home...

The three biblical commands to visit, care for, or heal a sick person are not contradictory but complimentary. Jesus entrusted these three mandates to His Church. He, who was never sick, identified himself with the sick, saying, 'I was sick, and you visited me' (Matt. 25:36).

Compassion, healing and conversion are three words often linked on the road to a person's salvation. How many of us were rebellious in a vertical position, but receptive when horizontal...?

Visits To Retirement Homes

"Do you have visitors from time to time?" I asked an aged woman, as I shook her hand.

"No, never... My son comes to see me for ten minutes at Christmas..." I said nothing, but I wanted to cry and scream at the same time for all those who die slowly, in almost complete solitude.

Perhaps that cry should be expressed here, for the thousands of grandmothers and grandfathers who, at the doors of eternity, desperately need the love of Christ manifested through you and me, yet no one visits them!

It is true that some of them never found time throughout their whole life for the Gospel or for its witnesses. However, as with the labourers in the last hour, God loves them and seeks them yet. The majority of them will accept your visit, your affection, your words, your reading and your prayers with tears of gratitude. Offering a ride in your car, or visiting them with your church choir, will be the event of the year for many of them!

Visits To Prisoners

'I was in prison and you visited me.' (Matt. 25:36) We were prisoners of sin, and Satan was our gaoler... and God, sovereignly, freely, came. In no way was He obligated to visit our rebellious planet.

Today, He is looking for those who will imitate Him, disciples who will seek and save those who are lost; in this sense, some initiatives can only be taken by you in your particular situation.

Paul Freiburghaus was in prison, declared by psychologists and psychiatrists to be a 'perverse person, inaccessible through education, insatiable, having given himself over to drugs for years. All judicial, medical and social interventions having failed to produce results, we recommend a relatively long period in a psychiatric institution.' Yet now, through his evangelism ministry, each year dozens of young people in Switzerland and elsewhere find new life in Christ.

Many other servants of God have been converted in prison, like the man who had already placed a rope around his neck to hang himself! He had tried everything: trips, vegetarianism, ascetism, drugs... He was standing on a stool, about to kick it from under him, when Christ found him and changed him radically. At that instant he remembered the phrase, 'I came to seek and to save what was lost' (Luke 19:10)

Drama, Mime, Choreography

How can you gather two hundred non-Christians in Switzerland in ten minutes, with no advertising, and present them with a clear message of the Gospel? Answer: by performing a drama at a lakeside on a busy day.

When we realize how much energy must be exerted to gain the same result indoors, we will turn to this method a lot more often (as a complement, not a replacement!). It also reveals Christianity in a new light, and enables innumerable contacts to be made. Do not wait to become professionals! God leads and encourages those who start out!

Sports

Paul became all things to all men for the salvation of as many as possible... One of the best means of reaching bowls players is to play with them; the same with tennis, volleyball, football, jogging, and so forth.

You can begin alone, like some runners who participate in popular competitions which are televised, and who wear a T-shirt with a Christian slogan. If you find a partner with the same objective, so much the better; you will be able to intercede together and strengthen one another.

Some will be able to form a complete Christian team. The aim will not be to win, but to be true sportsmen, glad of your strengths and conscious of your weaknesses, glowing with faith and creativity to share the Good News.

Camps

Whoever says sport, also says ski camps, sailing camps, hiking camps, etc.. I shall return later to the key role of the organizer who, let it be said in passing, could be a wretched sportsman, have a fear of preaching, yet be the catalyst for bringing dozens of teenagers, young people, couples, etc., to faith in Christ. In French-speaking Switzerland alone, it is at present one of the most effective means of bringing hundreds to conversion every year.

Choirs, Brass Bands

Our conception of a choir ministry is often too narrow. Every choir must choose and prepare its songs and, above all, do its annual planning, with an evangelistic perspective. A bag of salt set beside a tasteless soup does not do much good. Neither does a magnificent choir cloistered between four walls – at least, not for the sheep that are lost!

In a world that is informed in the extreme, those around us are all the more sensitive to a live singing recital, rather than a recording.

There were fifty of us. When our four-part songs filled the Palud Square in Lausanne, one would have thought the paving stones had suddenly been spread with superglue! Numbers of people slowed down, then stopped. The glory of the Lord was there... In two hours, up to nine people bowed their heads to make, or remake, that step to Christ. Song touches the hearts of the most hardened listeners, and opens the way for dialogue.

Why not perform at the next village celebration, at that wedding coming up, a national holiday, on Christmas or Easter morning, in the streets, the hospitals, the prisons?

During the wedding feast in Cana, Jesus was not in the synagogue lamenting over 'this world that's going all wrong'; instead, He was the light in the midst of the celebration... If Christ was the leader of your choir, where would He take you?

Courses In Music, Macramé, Pottery, Sewing, Languages...

The Mormons give free English classes to make friends, and to train people! If you have a gift, do not bury it, but make the most of it! Put an announcement in the newspaper, on the local radio or in your neighbourhood; one afternoon dedicated to this activity, and you have begun!

You can determine the details: the place (in your home or another's), number of pupils, and so forth.

In a little country village, a young mother opened her home for an aerobics course, and it soon became a great success on all levels. It was there that women, couples and children heard the Gospel.

Coffee Or Tea Debates

These are very much appreciated by high school and university students; a visiting speaker can be the reason, but it can also be done just as well among students meeting somewhere. Several African students organized some public debates, as in the Reformation, but this time between a Christian and a Muslim. In that situation, nothing really limits the number of listeners. The hotter the subject and the more seriously it is treated, the more people it will draw simply by word of mouth. Of course, it needs to be managed wisely, but with boldness, too!

Bible Study Groups

A simple recommendation: stay faithful to the calling of your group. Many non-Christians will come if the Bible is studied and they can freely express their doubts and questions. But they will leave if you include prayer, interminable introductions, and songs.

Do not lead the study as a teacher, but a good facilitator who listens to others, honours their input, and stirs excitement through valuable comments, without imposing a teaching. Sowing the seed will produce fruit, but it is useless to pull on the carrots to make them grow! Too many zealous Christians fail here, because they confuse Bible study with a fellowship meeting; people will be scared off and not come back.

Prayer Groups

Numbers have come to Christ by joining this type of group. These are often people who sympathize already, or who are looking for help. The groups that grow the fastest are those which have a clear objective, to welcome newcomers, who then feel that they were expected and that their presence is a little celebration for everybody. An active charismatic dimension – prayer for those sick or in difficulty (possibly followed by an appointment), the outpouring of the Holy Spirit, hearing the Lord's voice – and openness to missions and to the nations (as opposed to 'navel inspection'), correspond to a deep need for true spirituality among our contemporaries. If the occult sciences have millions of adherents, it is because of a super-rationalistic society on one hand, and a cold and timid church on the other.

Stickers, T-Shirts, Pins, Badges

It has been calculated that if your car is in a key position in a large town, a hundred thousand people will read your car sticker in one year. Choose the message prayerfully and according to your convictions, for example, 'I am a non-conformist, I read the Bible'. Even a small cross around your neck can begin a conversation, encourage someone, modify behaviour around you.

Would the world display signs of the zodiac, Buddhas, magnetic bracelets and all kinds of fetishes, and cover clothes and cars with enticing slogans, if the disciples of Christ passed unnoticed? Of course not! We are not to imitate the world, but that does not mean that we are simply to move out of the way and disappear! 'Shine like stars in the universe.' (Phil. 2:15)

Your Vehicle: Hitch-Hiking, Various Services...

Give to the one who asks you...

(Matt. 5:42)

Do not withhold good from those who deserve it, when it is in your power to act.

(Prov. 3:27)

The hitch-hiker is asking for a place in your car; of course, you need discernment, but also availability, for this is a form of hospitality. Take those on board for whom you sense a 'yes' from the Holy Spirit. Jesus sends us out in the midst of wolves, while asking us to be wise! (cf. Matt. 10:16)

Is it necessary to evangelize every person who gets into your car? No; guilt is a bad counsellor. Do we always have to be available to the Holy Spirit? Yes, but how? Keep relaxed, happy to respond to a need. Take an interest in the person and get to know him. If that is as far as the conversation goes, accept it; if it goes further, be a good but earnest witness. In saying goodbye at the end of the trip, I systematically offer a *cassette of a particularly powerful testimony*, which I have recorded myself, or a tract.

If you feel this ministry suits you:

- Surround it with prayer: for people, places, time, conversations and so forth.
- Make the place welcoming and prepare material of quality (tracts, cassettes, your visiting card or useful addresses).
- Be discerning.

In some places, drivers are sought after for the annual outing of elderly people... There are all sorts of possibilities for Christian drivers – they are precious!

Open-Air Work

This subject is treated in depth in my second book, *Porteurs de Vie* (in French only). It is a method of proclamation that was used a great deal by the apostles and by Jesus Himself. Basically, it is a matter of the Church 'going' to the world, and no longer being content with saying to the world, 'Come'.

In the streets of Lausanne during Easter of 1990, we noticed that people crowded to watch the 'King's Kids' performing, but they quickly dispersed the moment it was over. In order for this not to matter, we *stopped* all public commentary (before and after the production) in order to be among the crowd *during* the performance. thus making contact without any delay. Dozens of interesting conversations followed.

On another occasion, I was preaching, and by previous arrangement, a friend of mine set himself in the crowd and interrupted me, loudly disputing the message (thus acting as a spokesman for several listeners). I responded to a few of his objections, then invited him to call upon God to change his life. He came to the microphone and testified that he had already done this and that God keeps His promises. He then added an appeal. A young girl came forward, kneeled down and committed her life to Christ. This is a 'shock method' for a spiritually lethargic society!

Personal Contacts

In 'Youth With A Mission', we talk about 'divine appointments'. Almost every method explained here ends with some personal contact. On the other hand, the Christian who prays and expects people to cross his path who have been prepared by the Holy Spirit, will not only see his prayers answered, but will be amazed at the ways of God.

You could begin a journal of 'prayers and contacts' with the objective being one 'divine appointment' per week. As you add people little by little, they should be surrounded by persevering intercession. Who knows if the Lord would not lead you the way He led Philip (Acts 8:26-40)? Obeying the Lord's voice, he went out and met up with a man who had travelled four thousand kilometres to come and worship God!

Inspired words, and even words of knowledge and wisdom, can accompany the ministry. This kind of contact will normally happen in such a natural way, that it will only be in retrospect that you will marvel at how the Holy Spirit's methods work.

Door-to-Door Visiting

In Argentina, a young New Zealander went to the door of a large family's house one Saturday afternoon. The mother rudely sent her away. The following Saturday, the girl appeared again at the door and was rejected as before... Who among us would have gone to that door for a third time? This girl did. It was such a hot day that the housewife invited her in and gave her a glass of water – and was then converted, along with her five sons! They are all serving the Lord today. In fact, one of them is Juan Carlos Ortiz, the pastor of a church of three thousand members, author and popular speaker on several continents. This is not something that happens only to other people!

There are many advantages to door-to-door visiting:
- People are in their own homes, are natural, feel safe.
- They can easily be followed up.
- It is one of the best means of systematically reaching a neighbourhood, a district, etc., that is, proclaiming the message to every creature.
- If it is well prepared and announced in advance, the visit is expected by a significant percentage of the population, who have often not seen the pastor or priest for years.

Many people, confined to their apartments, like the alcoholic woman in her seventies who invited us in and was converted, will not have other opportunities to hear the message of salvation.

Do we still have compassion for the crowds without a shepherd? Are we still disciples of the One who accepted obedience in the face of opposition and blessing? Or shall we let our town perish without Christ?

Thirsty one day after several hours of going door-to-door, I asked my partner what she would like as refreshment.

"A glass of lemonade," she answered, and then added, "and a few biscuits with it would be nice." When we rang at the next door, a couple invited us in and offered us... lemonade and biscuits! As we were about to leave at the end of our visit, they expressed their astonishment.

"It's strange, but normally we don't invite in people like you."

Some time later, I was in a similar situation, this time with a very young convert. I told him the above story and asked him what he would like.

"Apple juice," he answered, and I added, "Mocha ice cream." However, the afternoon came to an end without seeing it happen. But the following day, we were offered 'afternoon tea' – of apple juice and mocha ice cream! These little 'winks' from Jesus showed me that He likes to stand at the door and knock. What about you?

Restaurants, Cafés, Christian Coffee Bars

Thousands of businessmen throughout the world receive the Gospel during a meal; thousands of youths have received it in Christian coffee bars; thousands of women discover it through 'breakfast meetings'.

One of our friends, who had moved shortly before to a small village, began this ministry from nothing. At the first breakfast, more than a hundred and fifty women came, from eighty-two villages! There is no doubt that such a method really corresponds to a need.

The Holy Spirit leads His people in this way because a meal makes an excellent environment, a proof being the high number of biblical reports of Jesus practising His ministry around a table. It is for good reason that He compares the Kingdom of God to a feast, knocks at the door to dine with us, and assures us that, at the resurrection, He will drink new wine with us in the company of Abraham!

Without necessarily opening a coffee bar or starting a 'chapter' of businessmen (yet, why not?), you can use a birthday, a meeting with old school friends, or simply the desire to give pleasure to your neighbours who never take the time for a little 'extra', to invite them over for a meal.

Listen, express your friendship, and Jesus, through you, will continue His work...

All These Ministries...

Can be combined almost to infinity. Think of that girl who, earlier on, did your course in macramé, then came to dinner at your place with her boyfriend. Two months later, they came to Bible study, 'just to see what it is...' Today, they are missionaries in Chad... Is that optimistic? Perhaps, but was it not through the same kind of process that most of us found Christ?

Imagine if *all the members* of a church got involved in evangelizing, alone or in groups, *one evening a month*, instead of having a meeting... One word of command: complete liberty of method, total involvement by everyone!

How many people would be reached?

How many members would be added to the church each year?

How refreshing and stimulating it could be for all the other meetings!

5.3 And What About the Finances for all This?

As this vital question is also linked with follow-up work, it is dealt with in detail in Chapter VIII (pages 137-140 below). But let us look at one last ministry, which is as rare as it is precious:

The Organizer

God has given to His Church a very large number of anointed ministries in all areas. I want to share a basic principle, but one which sometimes escapes us completely; it is summed up in these words: 'You do not have, because you do not ask' (cf. Jas. 4:2b).

As incredible as it seems, 95% of all servants of God throughout the world would truly be willing to come and minister in your area if you were to invite them!

I have so often heard Christians complaining that they do not have any good speakers and they reproach us for keeping them for ourselves. I then explain how to obtain these speakers: just pick up the telephone or a pen and ask them to come!

After having myself invited speakers from every continent, I can assure you that there is no magic formula, but a very simple truth: *speakers go where they are invited!*

I asked Floyd McClung (former international executive director of YWAM) if he would be willing to come to an evangelism campaign for four hundred people; he answered that he would be happy to come, even for one hundred non-Christians. Luis Palau, whom I interviewed for five minutes in Manila, pre-empted my invitation by saying that for a long time he had been waiting for a chance to come and evangelize in and around Lausanne.

Christian athletes, cosmonauts, singers, ex-criminals, scientists, politicians, concentration camp heroes, exiles, doctors, people who have died and been brought back to life, people who testify of the grace of God from their wheelchairs or those who have miraculously left them, 'ordinary' Christians... they are all there, a multitude of them, *at your disposition*, awaiting *your invitation*! The problem is not on their side...

Most of us are:
– Too spiritual (If it is right for that person to come, he/she will come anyway).
– Too complicated (Immense organization would be necessary).
– Too unbelieving (He or she will never come here).
– Too affected by complexes (We are not important enough).
– Or... too lazy!

But I beg you today, as I write these lines, if you feel that nothing is happening in your group, that yours is a forsaken area or country and you are cut off and isolated, *invite the Body of Christ to visit you, be the open door into your village, town or region*. So then, pick up your telephone or your pen!

Two simple principles to keep in doing it:
a) Honour the person or people invited:
– By clearly indicating from whom the invitation comes and what
    its goal is.
– By creating a structure that will aid in exercising that ministry.
– By anticipating appropriate honorariums and the reimbursement of travelling costs. However, most speakers from the West are willing to cover part of their own costs, once or twice a year, if they are going to a developing country. You do need to be clear on this subject in your invitation; taking responsibility for even a small percentage of the costs is a positive sign of commitment.

b) If necessary, draw people around you who:
- Love evangelizing.
- Take on part of the organization.
- Have good sense and a contagious faith.

DETACHABLE PAGE TO RECORD
PERSONAL REFLECTION

Summary of Chapter V, Using Your Talents For The Harvest

Adaptable Methods

Everyone can find a 'shoe that fits':

Hospitality	Library	Tea debate
Slide evening	Children's club	Bible study
Video evening	Crèche, babysitting	Prayer group
Correspondence	Visiting sick	Car stickers
Answering machine	Retirement homes	Hitch-hikers
Telephone, fax	Prisoners	Open air
Calendars	Drama, mime	Personal contact
Bible distrib.	Sport	Door-to-door
Book stand	Camps	Restaurant, cafes
Newspaper articles	Choir	Organizer
Local radio	Various courses	

What are the three methods of evangelism to which I feel called?

a) _____

b) _____

c) _____

What are the practical resolutions that I am making today?

_____

_____

_____

When shall I begin my first activity? _____

If I have a spiritual responsibility (pastor, youth or small group leader, Sunday school teacher, etc.): how can I put my church or group to work?

_____

_____

_____

_____

_____

Chapter VI
A Tool for Better Communication

A missionary home on furlough after a three-year absence, was asked to speak in the church that had sent him into the field. The pastor telephoned and presented him with three questions which he would be asked publicly in the meeting the following Wednesday. He would be given fifteen minutes to respond to each one. These were the questions:

- What is the most difficult moment you have gone through, and what would you like to share with us so that we, as your spiritual family, can understand you?
- What has been the greatest joy in your ministry over these last three years?
- What is your 'dream' for your next period in the mission field?

At the end of the meeting, the man was weeping...

"I have never in my whole life," he said, "had an opportunity like this evening, really to share from my heart. I know now that you have understood my work, I feel 'one' with you, and I'm ready to go out again!"

6.1 Asking Good Questions, at the Right Level

Asking questions, good questions, is so fundamental to communication, and particularly to evangelism, that we are going to dedicate an entire chapter to the subject. There are few matters so easy to learn and to practise on the spot.

Here is the way I learned. I was in Amsterdam following a course for leaders with fifty other students, among whom were several families. After two months of communal living, I still had not managed to establish contact with everyone, and even less so with the children. I could have explained this away by pointing out that, with the number of participants crossing paths, it was like living in a beehive; yet, for me, it was my inability to communicate with the children in an adequate way that concerned me.

I would ask them this sort of question: 'Did you have a good time at school this morning?', 'Is your teacher nice?', 'Do you like your new school?'

The answers given accordingly – 'Yes, it's all right,' or 'No!'– invariably had the same result: the conversation ended, and so did the relationship.

One morning, a specialist in biblical management and communication taught us how to ask good questions. This was an impressive teaching, and I decided to put it into practice without delay! So, while standing in line for lunch, I asked a little girl of nine, "What was your favourite lesson this morning?" I found I had gained the right to a full explanation, which went on through the whole meal. Amazed but pleased, I had a real shock the next day when, at a bend in the hallway, the same child caught sight of me and ran up to hug me!

Was I on a course on communication or on the gift of miracles!

6.2 What is the Key?

In the midst of my efforts to understand, the Lord intervened to ask me a good question Himself:

- What message did this girl receive in the depths of her heart when you asked her that question?

This is the list that slowly came to mind:

- My life interests him.
- He has time for me.
- He can learn something from me.
- He wants my friendship.
- He is at ease with me.
- I have value...

If ever there was a powerful message, this is one! Let us emphasize that it is in no way necessary for the person questioned to express what he feels, neither does he have to receive some special teaching. His age, social background, culture, is of little importance, for the message goes from heart to heart.

Who among us has not looked forward for a long time to some evening with particular friends, only to find our feelings mitigated after all, and left with that dissatisfaction that too often comes after a superficial conversation? At other times, the opposite happens: it is a time of warm fellowship and the friendship is deepened.

Is this really so mysterious? Do we in fact contribute to such circumstances? Allow me to make a suggestion: we too easily leave to the improvisation of the moment what could be prepared and meditated upon with the help of the Holy Spirit beforehand.

One good question which *honours* the other person by allowing him to *express himself freely* and *deeply*, can radically transform your time together.

6.3 A Specialist in Communication

Let us consult our communications expert, Jesus Himself, who, at the table just as on the road, in a boat as in a synagogue, would quickly come to essentials with His pertinent questions. I invite you to meditate on these for a few moments and discover the vital principles for yourself:

1 – Do you love Me?	(John	21:16)
2 – Who do you say that I am?	(Mark	8:29)
3 – Which of the two did what his father wanted?	(Matt.	21:31)
4 – Which... do you think was a neighbour?	(Luke	10:36)
5 – What is written in the Law?	(Luke	10:26)
6 – Whose portrait is this?	(Matt.	22:20)
7 – Which is easier: to say...?	(Mark	2:9)
8 – John's baptism – where did it come from?	(Matt.	21:25)
9 – Which of you... on the Sabbath day?	(Luke	14:5)
10 – Where are those who condemn you?	(John	8:10)
11 – Why do you call me good?	(Luke	18:19)
12 – Why did you doubt?	(Matt.	14:31)

Although far from being exhaustive, this list enables us to emphasize the essential characteristics of good questions.

A) The two first questions are:
• Very *simple* yet very *profound.*

A four-year-old child would understand them, yet they leave numbers of theologians perplexed! Our questions, on the contrary, tend to be complicated and superficial.

B) By the three following questions, Jesus:

• *Draws out the answer from the one who asks the question!*

The questions posed by His interrogators had focussed on obedience, authentic love and eternal life. With perfect psychological sense, Jesus teaches by asking questions in His turn. He thus shows that a good part of the answer is in fact already written in their hearts.

Let us say in passing that here Jesus also teaches us that true communication has taken place only if the principle can be related again by the person taught.

C) In questions six to nine, Jesus is speaking to His opponents. These questions are formulated in such a way that they:

• Require a *time of reflection.*
• Require *taking a position.*
• Ask for a *precise response.*
• *Reveal a divine principle.*

We are sometimes disturbed, even shaken up or thrown off balance, if the person remains silent once we have asked the question. However, it is often proof that there needs to be time for reflection.

In evangelism, one well-put question is sometimes worth more than long arguments. For example, if a Muslim asks how many times a day a Christian must pray, it would not be appropriate to answer by saying x or y times, because then Christianity would be perceived as being just one more religion. But if, instead, you were to respond by asking him how many times a day a son must speak to his father, the conversation would be on a completely different level: it would be about a living relationship with a God who seeks after every man, or prayer changing from monologue to dialogue... Thus a divine principle would be revealed.

D) The question that Jesus put to the adulterous woman would in some way 'revive' her.

Logically, her life should have ended under a volley of stones, condemned by God and rejected by her own people. It is worth noting that Jesus did not save her in contempt of the Law, but because He was willing to submit Himself to that terrible death in the woman's place. It was at this price that she arose, forgiven...

But let us return to the Master's question:

• It *puts a totally new light* on the situation. Here is an anecdote to help explain.

A factory which made bottles was on the verge of bankruptcy. An expert was called in in a last attempt at recovery. He asked the director,

"What do you make?"

"We've always made glass bottles, but we're no longer competitive and I don't see any way out."

"What are your bottles used for?"

"To contain whatever needs to be put in them!"

"So, you don't make bottles, you make containers!" remarked the expert.

That new light on the situation saved the enterprise: it continued to supply its clients with – containers, made with new materials.

Because we are used to our 'glass bottles', it is naturally difficult for us to adjust to new situations. But one good question, without pressure or manipulation, can be one of the finest gestures of love shown toward one's neighbour.

E) The two last questions listed begin with a 'dangerous' word, one we must use wisely, 'why'.

Of course there are the harmless 'whys' of little children, such as, 'Why are poppies red?' and 'Why do clouds stay up in the sky?'

There are also the 'whys' of the pupil or the apprentice who simply wants to learn. But beyond these examples, we must know how to discern an aggression that can turn against us:

- Why did you park your car here?
- Why have you cooked carrots again?
- Why did you answer like that?
- Why did you come back today?

- 'Why' often suggests a *rebuke*, a *doubtful questioning*, an *exhortation*, so know the reason for using it.

F) There is one common principle underlying all Jesus' questions:

- They simply draw the people to *express themselves*.

How can you have a conversation if a person remains silent? Those who work in evangelism will readily recognize that good contact with someone depends entirely at the beginning on a willingness to converse. Dialogue is often stimulated by the attitude of the Christian, which we shall study in a moment, but also by the quality of the questions asked.

- The words *which*, *what*, *who*, *when*, *where*, *how much*, which are frequently used in the Gospel, begin questions which cannot be answered by a simple yes or no.
  - What do you think of this performance?
  - Which evening would suit you the best?
  - Who do you think is the best actor?

6.4 An Analysis of Some Bad Questions

A) In contrast, these same questions begun with 'Do you think' or 'Would you like' evoke a yes/no answer from the start and can cut a potential conversation short:
- Do you think this is a good performance?
- Would you like to come to a meeting one evening?
- Do you think he's a good actor?

B) Those questions requiring a yes/no answer are not bad in themselves and are even necessary once a conversation has got off the ground. They must not, however, obstruct the flow or replace deeper questions. We need to choose them, rather than submit to them for want of imagination or creativity.

C) Asking two questions at the same time engenders confusion. The second one is often added out of insecurity, because of a silence after the first question, which is a pity... We need to have the courage of our questions. Here are some examples:

'Do you mind my interruption?' without adding, 'Would you prefer to talk another time?' or worse, 'Not very good, right?'

'How much would you like to give?' without adding, 'At least...?' or, 'Of course, if...'

'What do you think...?' without adding, 'Or would you rather...?'

D) Avoid questions that only confirm our own ideas:
- Isn't it true that...?
- I was thinking that...?

E) Or questions that virtually answer themselves:
- If I ask you..., you will no doubt answer...

F) A question that is too general can even be hurtful by the lack of interest it suggests, especially if the person who asks it jumps on to something else before the other has managed to get out his first word!

- So, has the year gone well? You're well, I hope?

What can you do when someone asks this sort of question, and you have so much to say? Take for example, an exciting trip, full of new experiences, which you have just made into Eastern Europe. You know that, at best, your neighbours will ask something like, 'It was Hungary, wasn't it?' And they will give you ten to fifteen seconds of their attention...

Keep in mind two or three particularly fascinating events that happened during the trip, that you can relate very briefly...

Surprised by the quality of your report, your questioner will usually continue the conversation.

Observe Jesus when He was questioned. His answers whet the appetite of His questioner. I am not saying we should 'force' people to listen to us, or should spout speeches at every opportunity, but I share this to help those who have trouble recounting events that are worth sharing with others.

These 'good answers' are an equally vital key to evangelism.

G) The questions to avoid absolutely are, in summary, those which make comparisons, are disparaging or contemptuous, those which are indiscreet, or which manipulate and force the other into a corner.

- Would you be able to get yourself out of this as well as...?
- Do you know what cleanliness is in this village?
- Obviously, it would be too much to ask that you...?
- What did you mean by saying you were embarrassed?
- So what are you waiting for before you...?

And Now, The Right Attitude

From the moment you ask a question of a person, you must allow him two fundamental rights:

1) *The right to reflect.*

The deeper the question, the longer this time of reflection can be. Sometimes, you will have someone exclaim, 'Oh, to answer that I'd need a week to think about it.' Sometimes it will be ten or twenty seconds (you cannot always assume how much), sometimes half an hour. If you respect this right, you will add a new dimension to your communication.

2) *The right to answer.*

Sometimes I am interrupted with a question such as, 'What do Christians do for society today?' Even if the person shows no sign of expecting an answer, I ask, 'May I answer that?' Surprised, the person usually says yes, in order to appear open to dialogue. I then ask how many seconds I can have of his time, and make the most of this brief attention.

Please, do not impose this sort of 'gymnastics' on the people you are addressing yourself, but:

- *Listen attentively to* and *right to the end of* their response, as if it was the only interesting thing in the world at that moment.
- *Show a true interest, a desire to learn,* to *build up* and to *serve* the other, keeping an attitude that is inspired by Christ.

6.5 What Fruit can we Expect in our Lives When Practising These Principles?

Learning to ask good questions puts new flavour into our encounters with others, provides a new tool for evangelism, and perhaps even adds new dynamism in our profession.

The quality of our friendships today has been sewn with the thread of the conversations of preceding years; in the same way, our future friendships depend on our present investments.

Asking a good question is often actually a way of planting the little seed that will lead to the landmarks of life: salvation, marriage, vocation. Take the example of Jesus, who one day asked His disciple, 'Peter, do you love me?'

As A Complement, Here Are Some Classic Questions Used By Journalists In Their Interviews:

- We do not choose our environment when we come into the world. Can you describe yours?
- In what way do you feel you are useful in your life / village / society?
- How did you begin at...?
- How did you get the idea / vision to...?
- What person has influenced your life the most? Tell us why.
- What for you is the height of misery?

- What for you is the greatest happiness?
- What is your motto?
- Who would you like to be?
- What is the strongest trait in your character?
- What do you most appreciate about your friends?
- What is your favourite occupation?
- What caused you to leave for…?
- Your sweetest victory? Your loveliest memory?
- What failure has particularly affected you?
- Do you have plans?
- And what is the situation like today?
- What do you find most difficult in life?
- Someone once said… What do you think?
- What do you do to relax?
- What makes you happy?
- How did you get this conviction?
- What quality do you prefer in men / in women?
- Who are your favourite contemporary heros or heroines?
- If you could change one (two, three) thing(s) in the life of your
- village / country / church, what would you choose?
- In your opinion, what is the main problem of…?
- How would you like to die?
- One last word: what is your greatest wish?

Summary of chapter VI, A Tool For Better Communication

To ask a good question is to honour, to value, to love...
Characteristics of questions Jesus asked:

- Simple but profound.
- Require reflection.
- Require a precise answer.
- One question at a time.
- Help to reveal a divine principle.
- Draw the answer from the questioner.
- Shed new light on the person or circumstances.
- Question the questioner, reprove, exhort, when necessary.
- Which, what, who, when, where, how much, are often used.

- Asking a question always implies, for you, an attentive ear, and for the other, the right to reflect and to answer.
- At the beginning, avoid questions requiring yes/no answers. Get rid of questions which disparage by comparing, are contemptuous, indiscreet, confused, and superficial.
- Even if you are asked tasteless and evasive questions, prepare intelligent and tasteful answers.

You have just returned from holiday. Imagine three questions asked by a friend which would enable you to describe it.

1. _____
2. _____
3. _____

A missionary returns home after two years in the field, and will come to dinner at your place tomorrow. Think of three subjects of conversation that would really interest you and that would honour your guest. What questions would you ask to introduce these subjects?

1. _____
2. _____
3. _____

Your church is organizing some door-to-door evangelism.
Prepare two questions to get on to the subject after the normal
words of greeting and introduction.

1. _____

2. _____

Chapter VII
God Wants Spiritual Midwives

"Do I have to get a big kitchen knife and open my heart to let Jesus come in?" asked a Swiss woman in bewilderment. A Protestant, she had long been trying to find out how to become a child of God, faithfully attending church since she was five years old. Yet, today, in her sixties, it was not the comparatively superficial questions about which she was uncertain, but *the* question, that of her salvation. Up until this point no one had been able to help her.

Earlier, the crowd had packed into the tent to hear the Gospel. Now, at her request, we had sat down together, while people lingered around the bookstand and discussions rose and fell in the coffee bar that had been set up for the occasion.

Probably disappointed numerous times before, the woman warned me from the outset, explaining, "I've already had hands laid on me four times and that didn't work; I neither have the assurance of being a child of God, nor of having eternal life."

Without hesitation, I replied, "You could have hands laid on you another two hundred times and it wouldn't change a thing! I believe in the laying on of hands, particularly for the sick, but I know that it is the Word of God that will lead you to the assurance you are looking for."

I opened the Bible at the first chapter of John's Gospel and asked her to read out loud the twelfth verse: 'Yet to all who received him [Jesus], to those who believed in his name, he gave the right to become children of God.'

The conversation picked up.

"How does one become a child of God?" I asked her.

"By believing in Him."

"Do you believe in Him?"

"Yes, I've believed in Him since I was a child. I know and I believe that Jesus died for my sins and that He's the Saviour of the world."

"What still needs to be done, according to this verse?"

"I need to receive Him..."

"Have you received Him?"

"No! Do I have to get a big kitchen knife and open my heart to let Jesus come in?"

When Jesus assured Nicodemus, that doctor of the Law, that he must be born again if he wanted to enter the Kingdom of God, he retorted, "How can a man be born when he is old? Surely he cannot enter a second time into his mother's womb to be born!" (John 3 :4)

This woman was asking the same kind of question as Nicodemus. However, she had evidently met several well-intentioned people from at least three categories:

a) The 'doctors of the Law' who had taught her everything about Christ, except for the one essential thing: how to meet Him...

b) The 'recipe givers' who had laid hands on her four times, thinking it would all 'just happen'.

c) The 'dogmatics' who used (very biblical) 'giraffe' jargon, in speaking to this sheep: 'You must open your heart to Jesus.' For her, that only suggested the 'kitchen knife' solution.

How many people today, in Switzerland, France, or your own country, would give their life to Christ if only someone were to show them how? One hundred, a thousand, ten thousand? I am thinking here of those who fear God or are seeking Him, but who are totally ignorant of how they can meet Him.

I talked about marriage to this woman! Eternal marriage with her Creator and Saviour. But, to be sure I was understood, I took the example of my own marriage. The conversation went like this:

"When I and my fiancée went before the justice of the peace, he asked me, 'Mister X, do you wish to marry Miss Y, who is here present?'

"'Yes!' I answered. He then turned to my fiancée and asked, 'Miss Y, do you wish to marry Mister X, who is here present?'

"'Yes!' she answered. But she could have said no. Would I have been married in that case?"

"No."

"But I said yes with all my heart! Yet, you're right.

The characteristic of a covenant is that the *second* 'yes' *validates the first*. God is all-powerful and He desires you for Himself as no one has ever done. The death of Christ means that He wants to purify you from all sin and give you a new life, and that He is preparing a place for you in heaven. He said 'yes' to you a long time ago; yet His 'yes' will never take the place of yours. The almightiness and the love of God can never fully move in your life until the day when you yourself, with all your heart, and aware of the consequences, respond with a 'yes' to the gift of His life, by giving Him your own.

"When I said 'yes' I 'received' a person into my life and I was never again alone: my young wife had come to live with me. This commitment didn't take more than five minutes to make, but it's valid for a lifetime. I didn't have to physically open my heart, but I 'received' my wife through a covenant, just as she also 'received' me. Do you want to receive Christ this evening by making a covenant with Him?"

"Yes, I do."

"Tell Him so, in your own words, and I'll just be the witness."

Very naturally, she invited Christ to take control of her whole life. She gave herself to Him... and He came and dwelt within her. The covenant made, we reread the same passage as before, and I asked her, "Have you received Him?"

"Yes."

"What, then, have you become?"

"I've become a child of God."

"How do you know?"

"It's written there..."

The next day when I saw her coming into the tent, I saw the light of the Kingdom of God on her face. On principle, I questioned her as to her assurance of salvation. Her lips gave me the same answer as her face. At the age of sixty-three, she had entered into communion with her Lord.

In this chapter, we shall study how to lead someone to Christ, but before we do so, let me share one more testimony that is no less astonishing than the above.

It was time for me to go to the hairdresser's. Normally, someone from YWAM performed this task, which made it a pleasure and rather economical! But that day, the voice of the Holy Spirit reminded me of my childhood hairdresser, as if it was there that I had an appointment. It was no extraordinary sensation, simply a thought which came with clarity and peace.

So, making use of a free weekend, that was where I went. The conversation developed quickly with this man who had cut my hair since I was four years old.

"You know," he said, "I've listened to Gospel Radio every evening for years."

"Have you ever received Christ personally, when they give an appeal on that programme?"

"Nobody has ever explained to me how to go about it."

"If you like, we could take a moment later to do it together."

"Yes, I'd really like that."

There were no other customers. The hairdresser closed his salon and hung a sign on the door reading, 'Back in a few minutes'. He could just as well have hung one saying, 'Closed for conversion!'. We went into an adjoining room and there, as we knelt together, he experienced God's forgiveness and reconciliation with Him.

I saw him several times after this; one of his friends, a pastor, gave him further counsel, and later, after a few years of retirement, he died in faith and peace.

This is a lovely story, but it also gives food for thought. Being familiar with his circumstances, I know that this man had for many years cut the hair of dozens of committed Christians, and even several pastors...

Are we afraid of the act of conversion?

Do we think that nobody wants to be converted anyway? Or, more simply, do we politely withdraw because we do not know what to do when someone is ready?

The evangelist Billy Graham writes thus in his tract, *The Assurance of Salvation*:

> One day, on arriving at a university for a conference, a student came up to me and said, "Mr Graham, please don't let us fall." I was astonished at his remark and asked him what he meant. So he added, "Tell us how we can find God. That's what we need." Another time, when I was speaking at a large university, a student declared, "We hear a lot of talk about what Christ has done for us, the value of religion and what personal salvation is, but no one tells us how to find Christ."
>
> I became burdened over these requests coming from sincere students and, ever since then, I have tried in my sermons to explain simply and clearly how to find Christ. Millions of

people today accept the fundamental elements of the Christian faith without question. However, innumerable are those who, like heathens, are ignorant of the way of salvation as it is taught in the New Testament.

7.1 How to Lead a Person into New Life

The study below answers the following question step by step: 'What do I do when I find myself with someone *desirous of coming to Christ*?' You will need your Bible as a 'working tool'. Put it beside this book, and look up the verses which I shall mention.

This method is based on using an open Bible in your conversation. We shall go through six verses or passages to learn how to use them in leading to Christ someone who wants to make a commitment to Him.

One of the many advantages of this way of proceeding is that the person is not receiving our 'good ideas', but discovering for himself, sometimes in his own Bible, the way of salvation. His faith will then be directly rooted in what God says, and in the days following his conversion, he will be able to go back to that on his own, without any difficulty.

We are going to imagine a conversation with a certain person, taking several simple questions as examples of those likely to be used in such a situation. They let us know if the interested person is understanding well. I have added the most common answers, in order to best familiarize us with the situation.

Make sure the person has the time (twenty or thirty minutes are usually necessary), then, after explaining why it is important to be in direct contact with The Book, find the appropriate passage and, as far as possible, encourage him to read it himself.

Now take the time to look very carefully at the given verses, because the questions asked are closely related to them. In reality, people sometimes take longer to answer correctly than I record here, but what is important is to lead them to find the answers in Scripture and not from 'common belief'.

In the course of this dialogue I have added in brackets some practical counsel for the reader. The letter A signifies you, B the person wanting to become a Christian. I leave to your own imagination the beginning and end of the dialogue.

A	Let's turn then in the Bible to Romans 3:23 and read that.
B	*For all have sinned and fall short of the glory of God.*
A	Do you understand what sin is in the eyes of God?
B	Yes, to kill, steal, speak wrongly about others.
A	That's true, all those things do offend God, but we could summarize them by saying, it's to live as if God didn't exist... Who have sinned?
B	People.
A	Do you think you're one of them?
B	Yes.
A	If we look at what God makes, for example, a sunset, the wing of a butterfly or the smile of a child, something tells us that God must be wonderful, intelligent, powerful, wise... And yet, sometimes we experience distress, loneliness, anguish, which are all a long way from inner beauty and harmony. Why is there this difference? Because our sins have cut us off from the glory of God.

Suggestion to the reader: write 'Rom. 6:23' in the margin of your Bible beside Romans 3:23. Then all you need to do is remember the first reference in order to find the five following ones.

A	In this same letter, which was written by the apostle Paul, the first part of verse 23 in chapter 6 is the second passage I'd like you to read.

It is important to help the person find the passage and, if necessary, indicate it with your finger in order to avoid his being embarrassed.

B	For *the wages* of *sin* is *death...*
A	We have seen that all people have sinned, and here we see the actual and eternal consequence of that... Do you understand why the word 'wages' is used?
B	Is it perhaps because it's something that is earned?
A	Exactly. Because God is just, He can never and will never be able to close His eyes to the evil we have committed. We alone are responsible for it. He must give us what our sins deserve. Death here does not only signify what we see in cemeteries, but just as much a breaking of relationship, first, with God, and

secondly, with others, through things like slander, jealousy, suspicion. (Sometimes relationships become so poisoned that we hear, 'For me, you no longer exist, you're dead!')

Thirdly, relationship with yourself is broken, because we do what we don't want to do, and we don't do what we want to do. Besides, heaven would become hell if God allowed sinners there, and anyway, not one of them would be able to bear the holiness of God. Therefore, there is eternal separation and lostness for those who don't want Him, and physical death is just one aspect of that.

That's bad news, but in verse 8 of chapter 5 there is a solution which I'll let you find, as the Romans did two thousand years ago.

Suggestion to reader: write 'Rom. 5:8' in the margin of your Bible beside the Romans 6:23 passage.

B	But *God* demonstrates his own *love for us* in this: *While we were still sinners, Christ died for us.*
A	Has God rejected you because of your sins?
B	I think… I don't know.
A	What does God feel for you?
B	He loves us… Does He love me?
A	Yes, as no one has ever loved you before. Our faults haven't provoked God to reject us, but He longs to forgive us. There's a true story which should help you to understand this love. In the army, some young recruits were learning to throw grenades. While the instructor had his back turned, one of them hid a grenade in his pocket, and that evening pulled it out in the dormitory in front of his admiring companions. Was it to show off, or out of clumsiness? Whatever it was, the young man took out the pin, took fright and dropped it.

Having worked with the weapon the whole day, all the soldiers in the dormitory knew two things: first, nobody had the time to get out; secondly, it was powerful enough to kill them all.

At that moment, one young man threw himself flat onto the grenade and it exploded immediately. His mangled body acted as a shield, and all the others' lives were saved! This is what Jesus, the Son and envoy of God, did for you and me: He took the grenade of our sin, this sin that we have committed and that every day we carry closer to death and just judgement. Christ gave His life willingly and died in our place in order to offer us total, free forgiveness.

Jesus' death on the cross perfectly reconciles these two truths: God is just and God is love. Thanks to this sacrifice, God can consider us as never having transgressed a single commandment. Do you understand that?

B Yes, I understand better. But what do I need to do, what is my responsibility now?

A Let's look at the answer to that in Acts, chapter 17, verses 30 and 31.

Suggestion to the reader: write 'Acts 17:30-31' in your Bible, next to the Romans 5:8 passage.

B In the past *God* overlooked such ignorance, but *now* he *commands all people everywhere to repent*. For he has set a day when he will judge the world with justice by the man he has appointed. He has given proof of this to all men by raising him from the dead.

A What is the response that God wants?

B Repentance.

A Of whom is He asking this?

B Everybody.

A When is the best time to do it?

B Now.

A Do we need to go to some particular place to commit ourselves to walk with Him?

B No, I don't think so.

A You're right, because it's written, 'everywhere'. God is everywhere, so you can be reconciled to Him *here* and *now*. He who made our eyes sees you at this moment. He who made ears hears you. He also created the mind and heart and He understands you.

But before making this step, which is, in fact, the most important in your life, I'd like to make sure you understand its full meaning.

Suppose my cellar is filled with rubbish and broken glass accumulated over years, smells mouldy and is badly lit. If someone one day comes to me wanting to buy my cellar, I can sell it and give him the keys in an instant. Now, this new owner will spend quite a time making the cellar clean and attractive, well-lit and useful. I can imagine visiting it some time later, and not being able to believe my eyes!

Today, you are going to change 'owners'. It is He who created you and bought you back at a price by the blood of Jesus, but it's you who hold the keys to your entire life. Up until now you have been the master of your own life and you can stay that way, because God is looking for sons and daughters, not slaves, those coming to Him willingly, and friends, not people who are divided or just resigned.

If you give Him your life, He will change everything: your goals, your way of thinking, reacting, deciding, of handling your relationships, your finances... It's a big step of faith, but it's the most beautiful thing that can happen to a human being. For we have been created precisely to base our lives on *His* wisdom, *His* love, *His* justice, which are qualities infinitely superior to our own.

In order to clean your 'cellar', God will ask for your active participation. He will lead you to ask forgiveness and to give forgiveness to others, to give up certain habits or bad relationships. He will guide you in what the Bible calls 'the fruits of repentance', but it all begins the moment you decide to give your life to Christ. That's what we're going to read now in Revelation, chapter 3, verse 20.

Suggestion to the reader: write 'Rev. 3:20' in the margin of your Bible by Acts 17:30-31.
Some believe this verse to be addressed only to the backsliding Church, and that it is not appropriate for evangelism. In that case,

you could instead turn to John 1:12, already mentioned, or John 14:23, which says, 'If anyone loves *me, he will* obey *my teaching. My Father will love him, and* we will come to him and make our home with him'.

B   *Here I am!   I stand at the door and knock.   If anyone hears my voice and opens the door, I will come in and eat with him and he with me.*

A   According to this verse, where is Jesus right now?

B   At the door?

A   This is an amazing picture, because Jesus reigns over the whole universe.   Yet He desires such close communion with man, and with you, that He wants to make your life His home.   What still needs to be done for your body, your life, to become His home from now on?

B   Do I need to ask Him to come in?

A   Yes, and God has made the invitation so simple that even a little child could express it, but many would prefer to enter into communion with Christ through their knowledge, their degrees, their own merits, and they fail.   Only those who know they are lost, wicked and poor, really receive it; they ask Him to fill their life and become the master of it.   Would you like to invite Him now, in your own words, to come into your life and take over its direction?

B   Yes...   Lord, thank You for loving me... for giving me life... for dying to save me from sin.   I ask You to forgive me for living for myself, as if You didn't exist.   Come into my life and change it.   I give it to You, it belongs to You.   You are my Lord...   Amen.

Suggestion to the reader: a few comments before continuing the dialogue.   Each prayer is unique, but, as ambassadors of the Kingdom of God, it is our responsibility to see that certain essential elements are present.   These are:

a)   An expression of faith in Christ for His work of   salvation.

b)   A request for forgiveness.

c)   A giving of the self by receiving Christ as Master.

Watch that the person does not say, 'I'd like' to receive You, 'I'd like' to belong to You, 'I'd like' to give myself to You, but rather, 'I receive You, I belong to You, I give myself to You.' It is not a matter of vocabulary here, but an expression of faith; we do not try to turn to Christ, but turn to Him! It is God who brings the new birth, but it is the sinner who turns to Him. It is vital from the start of his Christian life that the person does not ask God to do what God has asked him to do himself!

While salvation through faith is instantaneous, (a change of ownership), repentance and its fruits are a process: a change in thinking, then confession of our sins and acts of reconciliation and restitution. The criminal on the cross next to Jesus received salvation there and then, because his faith was real. However, it is certain that if God had miraculously delivered him from death, he would have tried to make amends for his wrongdoings, as Zacchaeus did. The person is saved by faith alone, but his faith will lead him to changes as deep as they are necessary.

A   Lord, thank You for the wonderful work that You've just begun in this life, according to Your promise, 'If anyone opens the door to Me, I will come in and eat with him and he with Me'. You've also said, 'He who comes to Me I will never cast out'. Thank You for this covenant that I have witnessed being established. In Your name I bless my brother (sister), and pray that you will protect him (her) by Your powerful hand. Amen.

There is great joy in heaven because one more person has given his life over to Christ, and you are the reason for this joy!

Prayer is as necessary to your new life as breathing is to your body. I encourage you to stay very close to Jesus in your thoughts. Allow Him to lead you in this process of change that we have begun together. I'd like to leave with you one more promise written by the apostle John. It's in his first letter, in chapter 5, verses 11 to 13.

Suggestion to the reader: write '1 John 5:11-13' in the margin of your Bible next to Revelation 3:20 (or John 1:12 or John 14:23).

B   And this is the testimony [of God]: *God has given us eternal life*, and this life is *in his Son. He who has the*

> *Son has life*; he who does not have the Son of God does not have life. *I write these things to you who believe in the name of the Son of God so that you may know that you have eternal life.*

A   Do you understand this passage? What are the gifts God has given to you?

B   He's given me... eternal life! He's given me Jesus, His Son.

A   How do you know that?

B   God says it Himself.

It is here that practical follow-up work begins, which is dealt with in the next chapter. The spiritual child before you requires all your attention, he needs a 'family' and it is up to you to make sure of that connection.

7.2 Some Comments and Suggestions to End this Study

* Meditate on the verses given until the Holy Spirit has woven a clear message into you, containing your own examples and your own questions. Expect Him to have you put it into practice soon!

* Be warm and natural. What you say is important, but so is the tone in which you say it.

* Do not be preoccupied with yourself, but let yourself be entirely taken up with the person; he must feel loved, listened to, understood.

* Reading with someone implies being close; be sure your breath is fresh.

* Sometimes you will meet up with people who know the foundations of faith well, like the woman I mentioned at the beginning of the chapter. You can then take just one passage and let it come alive together.

* If you are a counsellor in an evangelism campaign, the passages we have looked at can be useful as a complement, but be careful not to preach a message all over again! Rather, help the person to respond to and apply what he has just heard.

* The passages mentioned are short, but if we look at the context we see that they are in harmony with the whole; it is therefore not a problem to read the preceding and following verses. You can encourage the person to do it himself at home, by giving him the references.

* This method is a basic tool *for the precise moment when someone is ready to come to Christ.* You can improve it and modify it as you will, but be sure that, from now on, your role as a witness also includes that of a 'spiritual midwife'.

**DETACHABLE PAGE TO RECORD
PERSONAL REFLECTION**

Summary of chapter VII, God Wants Spiritual Midwives

- All over the world people are looking for Christ.
- Every Christian should, Bible in hand, be able to help such a person.
- List of references:
  Rom. 3:23,
  Rom. 6:23,
  Rom. 5:8,
  Acts 17:30-31,
  Rev. 3 20,
  1 John 5:11-13.

- Pray and prepare for this wonderful work.

Have I already prayed with someone to lead him to salvation? If so, how did it go? _____

_____

What are my inadequacies in this area? _____

_____

_____

What steps is God asking me to take to remedy this? _____

_____

_____

_____

If I received specific help at my own conversion, what three things did I most appreciate in those who led me to Christ?
1. _____
2. _____
3. _____

Chapter VIII

Follow-Up: The Key to Success

What pastor, or what Christian, has not dreamt at one time or another of new converts radiating the following qualities?

- Generosity and selflessness!
- Diligence in prayer and in learning from the Word!
- Appreciated by everyone (Christian and non-Christian alike)!
- Joyfulness and naturalness!
- Zealousness and fruitfulness!

This is certainly the description we find in the Acts of the Apostles (2:44-47).

But how did the first Christians get results like that from their evangelism?

What was the training programme offered to their new converts? We read about it in the preceding passage (Acts 2:37-42):

- They were cut to the heart (faith in the proclaimed word of God).
- They repented.
- They were baptized.
- They received the gift of the Holy Spirit.
- They devoted themselves to the apostles' teaching.
- They devoted themselves to the fellowship.
- They devoted themselves to the breaking of bread.
- They devoted themselves to prayer.

Many denominations and local churches strive to live out each of these points on the list (after all, they have been in all our Bibles for two thousand years!), but today there is a link missing between the second and third points: a great number of those who are touched and repent at our various evangelist activities somehow lose their way between that moment of decision and actually being 'added' to the local church.

This chapter is not focussing on doctrine (dozens of good books deal with the subject), but on the difficult practice of follow-up work, which often takes place today in an interdenominational context. The principles we shall study are also valid in the case of someone who is converted among those around you in everyday life. We shall concentrate, then, on the following areas:

- *Why are those who have believed abandoned?*
- *A first remedy: create an evangelism-follow-up budget.*
- *A second remedy: go and fetch the people at their own homes.*
- *How to prepare an adequate follow-up programme in an evangelism campaign so that the fruit remains.*

8.1 Why are Those who Have Believed Abandoned?

What would have become of you if, at your birth, the doctor, the nurses and your own mother judged your health acceptable, placed you on a shelf, and came back two months later to check on you?

You would be dead!

Would it be God's fault?

No, of course not, for He had done a magnificent job of preparing for months to come into the world, adding one cell after another, creating and fitting together members and organs, breathing life and character into this being, unique in the whole universe...

Would it then be your fault?

No, for the most advanced, strongest, most intelligent baby cannot survive in this world without outside help.

Then would it be the fault of those who brought you into the world?

Sadly, yes. And what a tragedy to think that those who wanted you the most, those who prayed for you with fervour that you would be born in good health, would now be those guilty of your death!

It works the same way with spiritual birth. If so many newborns are lost, it is not their own fault (although they do carry part of the responsibility), nor is it God's fault, but that of too many 'parents' who abandon their 'spiritual baby' on a 'shelf', for x reasons, expecting them to 'make it' on their own. And yet...

8.2 Fruit that Remains: It is Possible!

Jesus said, 'I... appointed you to go and bear fruit – *fruit that will last*' (John 15:16).

For years I wondered how Jesus could require of us that the fruit remain, until one day I understood and accepted that my responsibility did not stop at the appearance of fruit, but at its establishment. Jesus calls it 'your' fruit.

He asks it of us because He Himself did it before us. At the end of His earthly ministry Jesus could say to His Father, when speaking of the disciples with whom He had been entrusted, 'While I was with them, I protected them and kept them safe by that name you gave me. None has been lost...' (John 17:12).

We need to recognize today that a significant proportion of people who have responded to the call to conversion (in various forms) disappear as quickly as they came and never become members of a local fellowship.

Some believers, when faced with this fact, simply refuse to go into the matter. They claim that it is not their department; only 'low-born' people fall back, they say.

Others avoid the question by hiding behind an example that may be authentic but is not representative, such as someone converted through their efforts who is now faithfully attending church in the antipodes...

And finally there are those who, perhaps in pride, never honestly look at the problem in their own ministry or movement, and so avoid putting themselves in question.

But there is a majority of Christians who, after being deeply involved in multiple forms of evangelism, sincerely asks the question, and grieves over harvests that are partially lost.

I believe that you who are reading these lines are among this number and that you, along with me, will put this question to yourself, in order to find the way to produce fruit that remains.

Let us look at the basic problem:

8.3 A Newborn is Wonderful – But Needs a Lot of Help!

Having ten people on the 'penitents' bench' is as wonderful as having ten babies cradled in a nursery! It is not there that the work ends, but *where it continues!* It is also from that point that a time of duress begins for the parents. Those babies do not understand that

134

they should sing on Mondays from five to six, and cry on Thursdays from nine to ten after the message! No, they have their own programme, they are hungry all the time, they are fragile, they wet their beds or your arms and are notably selfish. Yes, and when the parents have no more strength, time or money, they may well ask if they really wanted a baby, or if they had ever heard of such words as budget, planning, or, more simply, cradle.

Is my church (of which I am, indeed, a part) prepared to welcome, feed, change, care for, listen to, and teach these newborn babes? Does it have some strength left, some money, some time and ability to adjust? Has it considered this reception in practical terms? Does it have a plan? Does it contain 'parents'?

8.4 A Change of Mentality

If, following the last call in an evangelism campaign, the faithful look at their watches, yawn and head for the exit, congratulating themselves on the meetings that went so well and are now 'finished', and the counsellors (if they exist), after a ten-minute conversation, pat the 'repentants' on the shoulder and wish them 'good luck', in preference to 'have a good year' or 'see you in heaven', we will indeed reap the consequences of our non-existent, indifferent or rushed follow-up. What are those consequences?

A)   The fruit is very weak, in bearing with the effort expended.

B)   In consequence, discouragement and unbelief have developed for future campaigns!

C)   Evangelism progressively becomes the 'poor relative' of the church.

D)   False conclusions are drawn, which are equivalent to amputating the arm of someone who has a problem with his leg! In this category, here are some examples that are very much in vogue among evangelism committees and other councils of elders:

a) It is not, or is no longer, the time for evangelism.
b) The age of big evangelism campaigns is over.
c) The church is not doing well, it is not ready.
d) Our effort was not in the will of God.
e) And all the reasons that the discontent will devise, to preach their 'fetish doctrine'!

Although this type of reasoning is often accepted and even admired, it can lead churches and entire regions off in the wrong direction for years. Let us make it very clear: even if all the above-mentioned conditions were simultaneously in order, so that:

- Both the 'ideal time' for evangelism and the validity of big campaigns is recognized unanimously by the committee.
- The church is doing wonderfully well.
- God reveals His approval so clearly that donkeys begin to speak and big fish draw evangelists to the shore.
- On top of all this, the positioning of the chairs is changed in order to please Brother X, and announcements are no longer made over the microphone but circulated in print, to please Brother Y.

If all these conditions came together, yet, because of a deeply rooted and fatal tradition, new converts were abandoned at their birth, the loss of the fruit would be certain just one more time.

Let us begin by looking at a few attitudes that sap follow-up work of energy at its source. Then we shall see how this can be remedied both individually and collectively.

1) Ignorance

Some Christians (they are legion), in all good faith, have never had any teaching on what to do when someone is converted. They may have participated in hundreds of Bible studies, prayer and other spiritual meetings but, unfortunately, these excellent activities have not been seen as a means to better serve God, but as an end in themselves: 'I am doing the will of God, not because I have understood how to do it, but because I go to three meetings a week!'

These people do sometimes see conversions: perhaps on a holiday (the teenager under the next parasol), or even at an evangelism camp. They rejoice over it and testify in their church, which is proud to have such 'committed' members. But if you ask them what has become of these 'newborns', they do not even know their addresses! They do not realize that somewhere an abandoned baby is dying.

2) Laziness

There are other Christians who know very well that you 'should' follow up those who come to the Lord, but...

Let us call one or two of them 'negligent'. This kind of person likes to evangelize, and he prays for people to be converted, because he is a counsellor at evangelism meetings. But to follow up that chap who wept over his sins the other night would take time, and it would especially take an effort of the will to look up telephone numbers or addresses, organize an appointment or write a letter. Really, all that gets very boring... So he finds good excuses to do nothing, for example:

- He has already done all he can in his free time.
- He is a counsellor, not a pastor; what could he say to that chap?
- God called him to 'win souls', others have to 'take care of the rest'.
- If things went badly, this fellow could become a real 'drag' on him, or even a 'leech'.

His conscience, who knows why, is the only thing that does not bow the knee to these wise reasonings. But Negligence has a strategy, a real atomic shield to quiet the conscience: he prays!

Somehow, his prayer is made difficult because of what could be called 'a deaf conversation'! But in spite of all this, Negligence asks God to do what God asks of Negligence: to visit, to support, to strengthen, to bless, to encourage, to love... Listening to his prayer would lead one to believe that Negligence is an expert, but God is grieved rather than impressed.

Some Christians leave it at this point, until the next conversion, but not Negligence. After three weeks, he cannot stand it any more. He pulls out an old postcard from his desk and writes a few kind thoughts to the person in question. The person will never answer... Maybe he has moved. But Negligence has finally succeeded in quieting his conscience.

3) Fear

This is the favourite weapon of our enemy, because it is so often effective!

'Has God really said that He will be with your mouth, that He will be glorified in your weakness, that He strengthens you and comes to your aid?'

Yes! But the old serpent prevents us from entering the Promised Land by setting before us the fear of rejection, the fear of being incapable, fear of ridicule, fear which paralyses all initiative in the face of follow-up work, which he, the liar, makes out to be a complex science, reserved for the elite, from which we are most definitely excluded!

4) Fanciful Theology

Rather than making up a list of a good dozen arguments, which would be incomplete anyway, let us summarize a few of their characteristics:

A)   We do not need to follow up new converts, because the Holy Spirit takes care of them.
–   Oh yes? And who is the temple of the Holy Spirit?
B)   Those who are meant to be saved will be, with or without follow-up!
–   Well, Jesus, Peter and Paul did not know that!
C)   Follow-up work would create conflicts between denominations; let the new converts freely choose their own spiritual family.
–   Does a baby choose its family? It is an original idea, but many are not capable of it!
D)   God called us to reap, not to store in barns!
–   But if farmers worked like that, our civilization would die of famine.

8.5 A First Remedy: Create an Evangelism-Follow-Up Budget

The change must come in our own hearts. Our priorities are wrong or, at the least, unbalanced. Let me explain. In most evangelism committees, hours are spent choosing a speaker, dates, a venue, suitable advertising, etc.. A budget is planned accordingly, anticipating the preparation and the event itself. Things are done in detail with sometimes eight or even twelve sub-committees covering all areas...

"All areas, really? And the follow-up?"

"Yes, that's very important," someone will answer. "And a committee has in fact looked into the question."

"Fine, but how much is the general budget?"

"X pounds."

"And the 'follow-up' budget?"

"Well, ah ... the counsellors themselves will be responsible for the follow-up... We don't want to make our costs any heavier..."

This is a summary of a classic situation:

Preparation: 33% of the budget
Event: 67% of the budget
Follow-up: 0% of the budget

138

What connection is there between the budget and our hearts? Just this:

'For where your *treasure* is, there your *heart* will be also' (Matt. 6:21).

Surely Jesus proclaimed this truth in order to emphasize that we must cling to true values and not amass corruptible treasures, but He is also saying that our treasure, our investment, reveals our heart's true centre of interest. In other words, a budget in which follow-up work receives zero per cent shows that our hearts are not won to this cause.

We are like a vine-dresser who, working unremittingly in his vineyard, finally reaps a magnificent harvest, then immediately goes on holiday, leaving the crates of fruit there to rot. Yes, the vine-dresser did a fine job of cultivating and harvesting, but all that was only a means, the end being to make a profit, gain a salary. Our goal is not to work unremittingly in order to fill an evangelism meeting, listen to a wonderful speaker and have ten people go forward to repent; that is a means (excellent, but only a means). What is the goal? It is, of course, that the Lord adds to the Church those who are saved, and that as many as possible enter into the eternal Kingdom of God.

How do we change our heart?

Experience shows that a 'treasure' better distributed between preparation, direct action and follow-up, moves our centre of interest in the right direction.

The day we invest financially in follow-up work is the day we will pay much more attention to all its facets: in intercession, decision-making, energy, time, literature, etc..

So let us look at finances:

- On the individual plan. (Included in this first point is everything pertaining to evangelism, as a complement to the fifth chapter, 'Adaptable Methods'.)
- On the collective plan.

8.6 Finances on the Individual Plan

In my first years of discipleship life I practised tithing and giving beyond that, but the idea of investing for evangelism never crossed my mind. I was happy to distribute any literature that was provided for free, to take a friend to a meeting as long as there was no entry fee, drive someone somewhere as long as there was petrol in the tank, etc.. This was a 'child's' view of things, which could, if continued, act as a real brake on the advance of the Kingdom of God.

At one point, the disciples of Christ were to take no money with them, thus learning total dependence by faith. This was done precisely because God used other people who, throughout the whole journey, opened their purses to take the disciples in and feed them. Take note that, in the group around Jesus, there was usually someone who looked after the purse and opened it regularly to give to the needy (cf. John 13:29).

A tract is free for the simple reason that someone, somewhere in the world, has paid for it. In the same way, entry to something is free because a person or association has covered the cost. Giving the Gospel freely simply implies the *generosity* and *evangelism budget* of the person who offers it, God Himself giving us the supreme example, in the gift of His Son to us. Salvation is free for us, not because it cost nothing, but because God paid for it in our place.

How much are we willing to invest to offer salvation freely to others? A day's salary per month? This would be as much a sacrifice for the one who earns little as for the one who earns much, but what a joy to be able to say on, for example, the first Monday of the month, today I am not going to work for myself but to invest in the evangelization of the world!

On this principle, whatever a person earns, he would put aside about one thirtieth of his total wage, whether this is much or little. What a difference this would make on the practical level! Almost all the examples in chapter V require some outlay to start off, except for a few which finance themselves or bring in a profit.

Although today I live 'by faith', I enjoy great financial freedom as far as evangelism is concerned, whether it is inviting someone out for dinner or a trip to the mountains, driving him somewhere, giving him a book or cassette, or for any other expenses in relation to his salvation or strengthening in Christ. Of course, this does not mean that I make a dependant out of the person newly converted, or about to be, or that he himself does not share in some expenses, but it does mean that my finances are now in the service of the Gospel, and no longer an obstacle to it. Did not Jesus speak of using worldly wealth to make friends for eternity? (cf. Luke 16:9)

8.7 Finances on the Collective Plan

Every president and every member of an evangelism committee, every director of a discipleship training school in YWAM or elsewhere, should understand that the final goal of an evangelism campaign is the growth of the Church. While the means to accomplishing this, such as the speaker, location, advertising, etc., must remain on the list of our priorities, the follow-up work is no less the keystone, indispensable to the success of the project. Once this is understood, the budget can be decided on. Of course, it would be ridiculous to suppose that this investment alone will ensure success; it is only a servant to the event.

Here are a few questions to ask:

• How long (from the decision to integration into a church) will the follow-up work last, on average?

• What do we expect of the person being followed up, and what will be the costs per counsellor of

a) Transport?

b) Telephone calls, correspondence?

c) Meals or other shared activities?

d) Miscellaneous?

• How many new people do we expect?

• Are we going to give them something, like a book or cassette?

• How many counsellors shall we need?

• Are the counsellors willing and able to take on part of the costs themselves? Will they be consulted on the subject?

The answers to these questions and others you may add will give you a base from which to calculate and decide on your 'follow-up budget'.

8.8 A Second Remedy: Go and Fetch the People at Their Own Homes

Whatever method of evangelism was chosen, the new converts are afraid of coming into your place of worship (youth group, house group, etc.) for the first time. Why?

• They do not know where to sit.

• They do not know how to dress according to your customs.

• They do not know how to sing your songs.

• They do not know how to pray.

• They do not know how to find their way around the Bible.

- They do not know that they can ask.

They are indeed terribly afraid of the ridicule, rejection or judgement of others. They get a knot in their stomachs in the face of all these psychological barriers to overcome, and most of them simply give up, in spite of a real desire to join you.

Think about it for a moment: did you go into a place of worship for the first time without being accompanied? If you did, you are an exception and I congratulate you; but the vast majority of readers will remember being accompanied by friends.

Here are two personal testimonies experienced since the first appearance of this book (names have been changed):

Mrs Moundou, of Benin, has achieved a university degree; she is deeply touched by the salvation message and responds to it. The meeting I have with her is friendly and goes deep. At the exit we meet up with several pastors. It is decided that I shall go with one of them to fetch her for the service the next morning. Mrs Moundou is more than desirous to come but, not wanting to put us out, assures us that she knows the address and that she will be there. Unconvinced, I accept the arrangement. It is a mistake, and she does not come...

And yet:

1) This distinguished woman sincerely desired to join us.
2) She confirmed the fact freely and seriously in front of several pastors and the one who had counselled her,
3) Only twelve hours separated us from the time of meeting.
4) We had communicated openly and without manipulation, and she knew where to go.

But a biblical principle had been violated, that is:

It is the shepherd who leads the sheep!

Alex is thirty-eight years old and lives in Switzerland near the Jura Mountains. We know each other well, as we studied the same profession together. I often pray for him. Circumstances sometimes bring us together for a cup of coffee. His interest in a personal relationship with Jesus grows slowly. It is decided that one Sunday we shall go together to church. Alex (calming my apprehensions) enjoys the worship, message and communion right from the start. During the course of a year I take him along, at his own pace and when I am in the area, about a dozen times. One day, there he is on his own initiative. Now, two years later, he has been baptized, is a member of the choir, and regularly attends church services and prayer meetings, as well as courageously witnessing for his faith.

Let us note in passing that most churches would grow yearly if each person were to fetch from their own homes those who have been invited. We talk about this principle, we joke about it, we dream about it, but we do not do it! What would happen if we stopped being religious and started being practical and real?

Do you want this? Well then, take one person (child, adult, elderly person) to church next Sunday and accompany him or her with love. In the French-speaking part of Switzerland (to cite an area where people do not exactly scramble to get to church on Sundays), some fellowships have received up to five hundred visitors in one year, and from them have seen dozens of new converts become church members! It is a fact that the church service must essentially be of quality, but the mentality of the churches' members is just as important.

Let us now look at how to prepare and carry out the work of follow-up in an evangelism campaign. The counsellor will always be its mainspring.

How do you Prepare a Satisfactory Follow-Up Programme for an Evangelism Campaign?

What I present below is not intended to be exhaustive information, but simply the fruit of lessons learned 'on site' from many a failure, trial, pitfall, and some wonderful victories as well.

8.9 Before the Campaign: Training Counsellors

To be chosen as a counsellor, a candidate should have *a good witness* in his or her home fellowship, have *follow-up work in his heart* and *be good at personal contacts*.

While good counsellors exist, they are usually very busy people, so it is important to offer training that is both concise and valuable if we want their participation.

The location of the training times usually greatly influences the number of counsellors present. In a big city, it is wise to have an initial meeting in *several areas* and in *several denominations* (the teacher himself being the one who travels). Once the vision and the interest has been communicated, a second meeting can be arranged for all the groups of counsellors together.

The meetings should *not grow in numbers*, but should *be obligatory* to all counsellors who received the first teaching. If the organizers take the names of participants at the first meeting, they can give a roll-call at the second, and so distribute badges as well. If there is no control, the training will not be taken seriously.

The training must answer two questions and cover these subjects:

1. What must I do and how do I do it?

These are the questions that the instructor, who will sometimes be the evangelist himself, must answer. If we want to succeed in our objectives, it is essential that we remain absolutely practical. The counsellor must be able to answer the following questions:

- At what time and where must I be for the days of the campaign?
- Will there be a rotation (teams for every other day)?
- Where should I be in the audience (to avoid all counsellors being in the same place)?
- When exactly should I go forward – during or after the appeal? (Many appeals get no response because of lack of communication with the counsellors. Personally, I believe the 'shepherd-counsellors' should precede or accompany the 'sheep' and not vice versa.)
- Who divides up the new converts for counselling?
- Where do I go with them?
- How do you fill in the decision card? When and to whom is it given? (Those comprising three sections – for the counsellor, head counsellor and new convert – allow for better follow-up.)
- What do I do if the situation is beyond my ability?
- What do I give by way of literature?
- When should I make my first visit?
- Shall I be helped financially and how am I going to receive this help?
- What is my responsibility toward the person in taking him to church, while respecting his own choices in this?
- What are the possible meetings I shall need to attend after the campaign? Will that be with or without the new converts?
- Will my training be valid for other campaigns? (Some counsellors find it discouraging that no record is kept and for each campaign, instead of using valuable experience by making a

144

distinction between 'new' and 'old' hands, they have to restart their training from zero.)

2. What must I say and how do I say it?

The counsellor must understand the attitude expected of him; he is like the 'visiting card' for the whole campaign. However, it is not possible to transform the course into discipleship training or a Bible school (which many speakers try to do, losing sight of the real goal of the meeting); no, if the local church has not taught the Christian life in more than a hundred meetings per year, this is not the time to do it.

Very practically, on this second point the counsellor will be taught on the following subjects:

- Tactfully building a conversation based on trust.
- Leading someone, Bible in hand, to understand and accept salvation.
- Understanding, with a few simple questions, the need of the person who has come forward.
- Briefly explaining again or clarifying the message heard.
- Presenting the literature and explaining its use.
- Making an initial visit with, for example, a very simple Bible study on the first steps of walking with Christ.

The counsellor should understand and accept this commitment:

I am personally responsible for the new convert from the moment of his decision for Christ up until his complete integration into the local church.

8.10 During the Campaign: What Will Make the Difference

The English-speaking world is composed of many countries, with varying degrees of openness to the Gospel. However, the principles remain the same, so it is up to each reader to interpret the lines following according to his or her context. Simply be careful not to persuade yourself that your 'area' is the most difficult and that 'that will never work with us here', before having tried it!

For the YWAM campaign held in August, 1991, in Cotonou, the economic capital of Benin, we decided to put the emphasis on follow-up work. Since 1982, we had tried different methods in a dozen different campaigns, sometimes with bitter failures. The fact was that, for the most part, it was in the follow-up that one or two links in the chain were missing. Let us look at some key elements:

1) The Appeal

This must be precise and, if necessary, given in several phases. In Cotonou, Christians tended to come forward for various needs, mixing with those who were coming to Christ for the first time. The result? Counsellors were inundated by a mass of people, which seriously handicapped their work.

We quickly organized four types of ministry in order to execute and fully cover the work of the counsellors:

A) When the call for conversion was over and the counsellors had begun talking with people, the sick who were desiring prayer could come forward. As there was a large number of these, sixteen pairs of team members took the time to see them one by one in front of the stage.

B) Other team members, especially trained for the task, were in a tent where they received those who had some greater need, such as deliverance. People needing this ministry could be sent there from anywhere else in the meeting.

C) As the evenings continued, several people would bring fetishes and other occult objects which they wanted to get rid of. A few team members would pray, sing and rejoice with them around a cheerful fire!

D) All other team members simply remained with the crowd, ready to answer questions, give information, testify, pray, give directions and assist in any way necessary.

Please note that announcements on the microphones and music must stop at this point, so that serious conversations can take place. It is a quite deplorable situation if counsellors and those who have responded to the appeal are forced to shout in one another's ears. This can be a difficulty in every kind of contact and particularly when praying for the sick. Where in the Bible do we read about the disciples singing at the tops of their voices in Jesus' ears while He was praying for people? Unless there is evidence to the contrary, it is still Jesus, and not the number of decibels, who saves, restores and heals today! The value that we give to these contacts is also revealed by the atmosphere that surrounds them.

The preacher, or the director of the evening, must therefore understand these different elements and be careful to manage each one correctly His concern to see fruit which remains will again protect him from producing a movement of mass confusion. If the appeal goes out for everything at the same time, it will end in anarchy and render follow-up work almost impossible. In contrast, if the invitation is clear, the crowd will quickly understand that it is to their advantage to respect the various instructions.

2) Location

The place where new converts and counsellors meet, which we could call the 'maternity ward', is worth all our attention. It should be:

A) Sheltered from curious onlookers.
B) In a quiet place, favourable for conversation.
C) Well enough lit to enable writing.
D) Warmly inviting, comfortable.
E) Sufficiently large.
F) Equipped with a children's section.

An Argentinian pastor was reporting how the mentality had changed in his country in this respect. Today, those who respond to the call for salvation are no longer greeted with dusty areas backstage, badly lit and containing a few broken chairs. The Christians, even with very little means, prepare a tasteful location for these meetings. Low tables are set in a pleasant arrangement, decorated with flowers and providing hot drinks and biscuits. The seats are comfortable. It is a warm atmosphere that is favourable to deep ministry and to creating new friendships.

Is this really of little importance? Remembering how the father received the prodigal son will give us a very biblical idea of the welcome which God gives us as an example (Luke 15:22-24, 32). Even if we do things more simply than that, we can put our whole heart into it.

3) Directing

If the crusade covers a whole region, follow-up will be made vastly easier if the counsellor and the new convert live in the same neighbourhood or small town.

How, then, does one make sure that they meet each other within a few seconds in a large people group responding to an appeal? One method we have found as effective in Africa as in Europe. Inside the 'maternity ward', signs bearing the names of the different districts of the city are set up a few metres apart. As soon as people have come forward and left the auditorium, they are invited, with help if necessary, to go to the sign indicating the area where they live. That done, the counsellors divide equally those present from each area. For a larger crowd, some earlier signs are necessary, for example, the western districts to the left, eastern districts to the right, and then the names of the suburbs themselves would appear a few metres further on. This idea can also be applied for the children, with a special entrance for them and their counsellors.

The neighbourhoods closest to the location of the meetings will often be heavily represented; knowing this, it is important to have a larger number of signs and counsellors for these, in order to keep the groups evenly divided. If need be, this can be adjusted for the following day.

Let us summarize the advantages of this method:

A) Only a few props and signs are needed, but it will save hours of travelling and transport expenses, which the counsellors or the churches cannot always provide.

B) In the ideal case, a counsellor who attends a church in his own neighbourhood will easily be able to take the new convert along.

C) The counsellor and new convert will be able to meet again more quickly, more easily and more often.

D) 'Disputes' over which church the new converts should attend will be avoided, if each counsellor has the freedom (without pressuring, of course) to take them to his own church.

E) It would also be possible for the counsellors, by common consent, to go to the area, i.e. the sign, corresponding to their church location, if that is different from their residence, so that the new converts will not have to cross the city in order to attend church with them. Distribution of converts among denominations will not only be made in relation to the counsellor, but also geographically.

For example: a counsellor lives in neighbourhood A but is part of a church in neighbourhood E. During the campaign, he will counsel people from neighbourhood E so that they will integrate more easily into a church near them. In this case there will be more travelling expenses. What is important is to make the choice carefully before the campaign and to stick to that.

F) Fruit that remains will be more numerous and, because of that, evangelism campaigns will multiply!

4) Training For The New Converts

In Cotonou, we held teaching sessions for new converts every afternoon from 5 to 6 o'clock. The number of participants grew from fifteen on the second day to two hundred and fifty on the sixteenth and last day. Some came only once, others daily, depending on the date of their conversion and their availability. In all, out of a thousand decision cards turned in, five hundred people benefited from the teaching. It is not difficult to imagine that a new Christian will be stronger after attending a course like this, plus several evangelistic evenings, than after a single meeting with someone and no follow-up.

5) Visits To The Home

The best method is to see that these are made by the same counsellor. Why?

- The new convert is often not ready to trust any person other than the one with whom he had his first contact.
- If the counsellor knows that it is up to him to look out for the person, he will generally be more conscientious and practical in taking down the address and making an appointment.
- He will know better than anyone else where the person is spiritually.

We must denounce the practice, as widespread as it is disastrous, of piling the decision cards on a pastor's desk at the end of an evangelistic effort. This custom is the cause of real spiritual slaughter, the reasons for which are simple and dramatic:

- The pastor in question already gives 120 or 150% of his working time to his work; he will feel guilty but unfortunately incapable of assuming all those visits.
- Certain addresses will be incomplete, others illegible; rejection of this unknown person at the door or on the telephone will be frequent, especially if it is a family member who answers and not the interested person himself.
- The counsellors divest themselves of all responsibility and disappear into thin air, because a 'professional' has taken over.

So, then, each counsellor will make his first visit within forty-eight hours of the initial contact. This is where the great spiritual battle takes place and where the Church loses or gains a large part of her potential members.

A newborn baby needs his parents immediately, even if he does not know it!

This means that visits will often take place *during the time of the campaign.* Here we touch on the central message of this chapter; I should like it to be understood and I do insist that *a counsellor who is not totally committed to making visits should not sign up for this job.*

- Addresses must be recorded with military precision. In Africa, many streets have neither names nor numbers. Because of this, new converts give their box number, which is completely useless for visiting! In these conditions, the counsellor must have the address explained in terms of crossroads, known buildings, petrol stations, and so on.

In Cotonou, several counsellors would find out the addresses of people by accompanying them home right after the meeting. However, where family persecution is frequent, more care must be taken. Situations vary a lot from one case to another, so each counsellor will need to adjust sometimes to meeting elsewhere or even in his own home.

With these difficulties in mind, let us underline again the advantage of being a counsellor to someone from one's own neighbourhood or village.

The counsellor will go to the homes of his or her 'sheep' (one or more) for the first few Sundays to fetch them for church. If there are many of them, he can arrange a time to meet at a central point in the neighbourhood (200 to 300 yards from their homes). If one is missing, he will go to get him personally, entrusting the group to another assisting member, or he will return later to visit the missing sheep. Jesus could not have made it more clear in His teaching: a good shepherd must count his sheep (the devil says that is pride) and search for the one who strays until he finds him (the devil says you should leave him alone, he needs time to think). It is not possible to obey the serpent and the Lord at the same time: one wants to lose and the other wants to save. What will you do?

8.11 After the Campaign: No One Lets His Arms Drop!

- Intercession does not slacken.
- Visits continue.

- The new convert continues to be accompanied by the counsellor, as the occasions arise, to a prayer group, a youth group, and to the life of the church in which he is received.
- The whole church mobilizes itself to integrate the newcomers.
- The head counsellor supervises the smooth running of things, encourages, keeps the committee director informed, deals with possible conflicts. He can also plan meetings, decentralized or otherwise, for the new converts.
- A 'love feast' of thanks and welcome could be held, bringing together pastors, counsellors and new converts.

8.12 General Reflection

As mentioned before, this chapter is not a complete study on follow-up work, but a beginning. If you have an experience to share on the subject, write to me, as it could enrich a later edition of this book, and so help a large number of people with a similar burden. As an evangelist, I am personally available to work beside Christians committed to bearing fruit that will remain.

Let us so pray and act that a new mentality will inspire our evangelism and the harvest be brought in; the growth of the Church depends largely on this.

Conclusion

Be practical: detach and fill in the following page now, while your thoughts are still on what you have read.

DETACHABLE PAGE TO RECORD
PERSONAL REFLECTION

Summary of chapter VIII, Follow-Up: The Key To Success

- Do not abandon those who have believed.
- Creating an 'evangelism and follow-up' budget.
- Training counsellors before the evangelism campaign.
- Do not change the shepherd.
- Preparing satisfactory follow-up during the campaign.
- Fetching the people from their own homes.
- Following through with new converts until their integration.
- Pray and move toward a new mentality in this area.

What changes shall I bring to my budget in face of personal evangelism and follow-up work? _____

_____

What is my personal commitment before God concerning follow-up work? _____

_____

What changes seem essential for the next evangelism campaign in my region?

For counsellors:

1. _____
2. _____
3. _____

For my church:

1. _____
2. _____
3. _____

For my locality:

1. _____
2. _____
3. _____

Chapter IX

A Plea for the Small Half of the World

Is work among children only a minor part of the work of God? Listen to the opinion of a great nineteenth century revivalist, when he was questioned about his ministry.

"How many people were converted on your last evening?" he was asked.

"Two and a half!"

When he was questioned about the 'half', he explained, "Two children and one adult came forward at the appeal. The adult gave only half his life, as the first half has already gone by without Christ, whereas the children gave their *whole* life!"

Work amongst the young has incalculable repercussions: it is an *investment for the world of tomorrow*. It is a field ripe for harvest, not only capable of producing fruit that remains, but of multiplying to infinity.

Childhood is a privileged time to receive faith in Christ, but, paradoxically, it is the upcoming generation which is the object of shockingly violent attacks today. We must focus our attention on this challenge before us.

Investing in this area will have us touching on subjects as diverse as the family, school, the media, social work or the Church.

9.1 A Mission of First Importance

While concentrating on reaching the world, we can lose sight of the *potential* represented in the conversion of the youngest, even if it is a question of just one child coming to the Lord. The choice of his profession, marriage partner, and social, political and religious involvements will all be radically influenced by his covenant with God. Jesus declared with great wisdom, 'See that you do not look down on one of these little ones' (Matt. 18:10).

Are we aware that 42% of the world's population is under twenty years old, and almost a third is under fifteen? They comprise more

154

than two billion three hundred million human beings, through whom the *future of humanity* is at stake.

William Booth, founder of The Salvation Army, expressed it thus: 'What is important is the child, for the world of tomorrow will be shaped by the child of today.'

9.2 An Urgent Mission

In the same vein, a Christian 'sold out' for the Lord stated, 'It is clear that God wants to save people *as soon as possible*. Christ did not die on the cross for us to spend the first part, the greatest part, of our lives in the grip of Satan.'

He was confirming what the psalmist said long before, when he wrote, '*We will tell the next generation* the praiseworthy deeds of the Lord, his power, and the wonders he has done... that *they would put their trust in God*' (Ps. 78:4-7).

Yet today, we need only look at the news to realize the message has not been passed on; on the contrary, reports of violence and even murders perpetrated by children fill our newspapers. Drugs and dealing infiltrate our schools, teachers complain that they no longer have any authority over their pupils, and the rate of illiteracy among young army recruits both astonish and alarm the authorities. Even in villages, burglaries of various kinds, committed by youths, force people to security measures never practised before.

What is happening? Have we lost contact with those who are building the society of tomorrow? In some social spheres in France there has been absolutely no Christian faith passed on for three generations.

At the same time as this crisis in our society, an unparalleled scope of attacks has been set up to wreak havoc against life, education, faith, the family, and even the very existence of the coming generation.

A) Attacks Against The Existence Of Children

Claire-Lise De Benoit, pioneer of children's work with Scripture Union, was asked at what point a child is open for the grace of God. "From conception," she answered. "Evangelization of children begins with the evangelization of future mothers."

Statistics show us that while there is one chance in two hundred thousand of being killed by a terrorist in Europe, there is more than one chance in five of a child being done away with in the womb of his own mother.

Conclusion: because of the abandoning of spiritual values, it has become potentially much more dangerous to be in a mother's womb than to live in our society! It is calculated that close to *one third* of pregnancies throughout the world end in deliberate abortion, that is, *sixty-five million per year!*

A beautiful American teenager testified, "I am alive today because a nurse pulled me out of the rubbish bin where I had been thrown!" It can in fact happen that an aborted baby is capable of surviving. This means that a nurse can be faced with the dilemma of having a premature baby to save at all cost, and an aborted baby of the same age to throw away!

Man can develop wonders in ultra-modern hospitals but, without God, he falls back into the most primitive of pagan practices. Sacrificing to the 'god of freedom', we have reached the point of throwing children in the rubbish who could have survived in an incubator. Those who escape the massacre, like that young girl, are often deeply affected by feelings of being unwanted, rejected and unable to find a reason to live. They desperately need to receive this Good News message that no, they are not the result of an 'accident', God did not have His back turned when they were being conceived; He formed them, knitted them together, desired them in the very womb of their mother, and they are unique. A future and plans of peace are prepared for them to the extent that they decide to follow Him who gives Life.

But aborted babies do not always end up in rubbish bins: an unspeakable market has been organized for them. In India, for example, foetuses can be sold to professional abortionists, who, in turn, sell them to large, multinational cosmetics companies or to laboratories for experiments.

But what does the Bible say about the prenatal life of the human being?

'Before I formed you in the womb I knew you, before you were born I set you apart; I appointed you as a prophet to the nations.' (Jer. 1:5)

'Your eyes saw my unformed body. For you created my inmost being; you knit me together in my mother's womb. I praise you because I am fearfully and wonderfully made.' (Ps. 139:16,13-14)

'He [John the Baptist] will *be filled with the Holy Spirit even from birth.*' (Luke 1:15)

'When Elizabeth heard Mary's greeting, the baby leapt in her womb, and Elizabeth was filled with the Holy Spirit. In a loud voice she exclaimed: 'Blessed are you among women, and blessed is the *child* you will bear... As soon as the sound of your greeting reached my ears, *the baby in my womb leaped for joy.*" (Luke 1:41-44)

Where are we in defending the life of the children?

In the United States, Christian movements have been raised to offer alternatives to abortion, such as adoption, for future mothers, or support for those who desire it. They are also taking action to change the laws and grant the right to life to those whom the Bible calls children. Christian centres of this type are being established in many places, and we can save lives by letting these places be known. On the side of prevention, a video, *The Silent Cry*, was broadcast on several national TV chains, through an echogram showing viewers an abortion. This helped many people to realize that the embryo is in fact a human being who struggles and 'screams', powerless against the instruments which take hold of it and kill it.

'Rescue those being led away to death; hold back those staggering toward slaughter!' (Prov. 24:11)

'Speak up for those who cannot speak for themselves, for the rights of all who are destitute.' (Prov. 31:8)

Yes, we can become one of these messengers of life, or support them, even if the opponents react more and more aggressively against protection of life in the womb.

B) Attacks Against Their Physical Integrity

In Thailand, children may work twelve hours or more per day. In India, they are also liable to be used for forced labour from the youngest possible age. In Colombia, child slave trading was recently discovered. Kidnapped by drug traffickers, they had to work secretly in the jungle in poppy cultivation. At the age of eight, the child was exactly the right height for cutting the poppies, but at twelve he knew too much and was cold-bloodedly killed.

In Bangkok, a quarter of a million children are delivered up to prostitution to gratify the vice of adults, many of whom are from the West.

Even in our so-called 'civilized' societies, children's bodies are shamelessly exploited and made the object of lust for sexual maniacs.

In the United States, a quarter of the girls under seventeen have been sexually molested, and one in eight boys.

I remember posters in the Paris underground, printed by the Society for the Protection of Children (*Protection pour l'Enfance*). One showed a little girl of about twelve, dressed in a long white nightgown, and obviously pregnant. The caption read, 'Her stepfather loved her a lot, but the neighbours were waiting for proof... Interfere with what is not your business!' And another similar poster of a little boy of three or four with swollen face and a leg in plaster, bore the caption, 'The neighbours managed not to blink an eye, but they managed to close their eyes... Interfere with what is not your business!'

Faced with these terrible injustices, we realize how much the child needs our protection. And in the measure we know of offensive situations, we must stop them by reporting them to the competent authorities. Social services can then intervene and, if necessary, help children out of these pathogenic families.

But in face of the extent of the trauma affecting them, one understands how much these children would need inner healing. Only God can heal broken hearts, enable past things to be buried and all things to become new (2 Cor. 5:17). And these children must be put in contact with He who restores lives.

Carolyn Koons, hated by her mother, threatened with death by her father, found a reason to live because a committed Christian mother prayed for her salvation and 'pursued' her until she was converted. She became a radiant young woman and successful teacher, then adopted a little Mexican boy for whom she provides a normal life. She has authored several books, including *Healed From My Past*, whose title so well summarizes her life.

Our society desperately needs social workers, judges for children, educators, schoolteachers, youth leaders, who are also committed *Christians*. To be a *disciple* and be *committed socially* is not as impossible as we imagine. I myself have experienced being a social worker in the sleazy neighbourhoods in and around Paris.

Let us enlarge our fields of vision and pray that the Lord will call many to represent Him among the most disadvantaged.

C) Attacks Against Their Faith

Atheistic ideologies have fully grasped how strategic and significant young childhood is. In the former USSR, for example, it was strictly forbidden to give the least Christian education to children under eighteen years. As 95% of the mothers work outside the home, the toddlers were placed in kindergartens which were assigned to teach them 'correct' ideology.

In Cambodia, under the Khmer Rouge regime, children were indoctrinated and separated from their families, thus becoming easy prey for political instructors. They managed to get the children to denounce their own parents; the night was compared to 'a pineapple with a thousand eyes', as the little ones glided among the adults and reported everything hostile to the regime. Their denunciations were followed by tortures and executions.

Addressing his Protestant colleagues, a Roman Catholic priest reprimanded them severely. 'You people are wretched idiots! You leave the children in Satan's snare until they are adults, then you set yourself to reclaim them by force. We, in contrast, know that children are as malleable as clay in our hands, and we devote ourselves to them. When they are well-taught and trained, we know that we need not fear as to their future.'

Even among committed Christians, I often find adults who are reticent of evangelizing children. In their opinion, 'it's too easy', or else it seems too much like manipulation. Yes, it is true that children are very receptive, but if we as Christians simply fold our arms before a generation in search of true values, we will deliver them into the hands of the god of despair, 'life has no meaning', the money god, the sex god, the drug god – and the list goes on!

Would that not be calling evil good and good evil (Isa. 5:20)? And in speaking of manipulation, is that not exactly what is found in the abandonment of the youngest into the hands of a consumer, anti-Christian society? What excuses shall we conjure up when the Master calls us to account for this generation delivered over to false shepherds? Shall we be like those unfaithful watchmen who did not bother to send out a warning at the proper time? Will the blood of this generation be required of us (Ezek. 3:17-21)?

Let us understand the Lord's great indignation when He saw His own disciples stopping the children from coming to Him (Mark 10:14), and let us fulfil our calling by showing them the love of God, and His call on their life. Keith Green (the late Christian singer) and David Wilkerson (founder of Teen Challenge, an organization fighting against drugs) knew so well how to do this. May there be a multiplication of such ministries!

D) *Attacks Against Their Education*

Never has our consumer society offered so much to children. They have everything, and they have it instantly! In Sweden, laws have been passed forbidding parents to discipline their children, thus seeing the reign of the *laissez faire* type of education first advocated by Rousseau. This assumed that man was good by nature. The children are now eating the bitter fruit of the false doctrines that accompany the resignation of parental authority, with its dramatic consequences: delinquency, runaways, drugs and a steadily rising suicide rate.

Left to themselves, the children find *television* fills the *emptiness* in their hearts, with its procession of violence and anti-heroes (the gangster is placed on a pedestal!). Cartoons, too often bloody, present a world of 'super power' and could hardly be a better preparation for occultism.

Before reaching the age of *twelve*, a child will have watched an average of about *thirteen thousand murder scenes*! This does not take into account the friend's or big brother's videos, which give access to a whole world of pornography that is taken to be the sexual norm for adults! We see all the more how destructive it is when we realize that children learn by imitation.

The connection between violence and videos, long decried by psychologists, was made excruciatingly clear by the murder of little two-year-old James Bulger, killed by two children aged... eleven! The horror film *Child's Play 3*, watched by the murderers just one month before their irreparable act, shows how the victim is spray-painted before being mutilated on a railway track. The scenario was copied to the letter.

In the face of this tidal wave of filth, we must protect our children by learning to say 'no' when they want to watch programmes depicting violence, immorality or the occult. Having a selection of good videos can help you set up a system that will satisfy both parents and children.

More and more protests are being heard from parents who are finding such violence unacceptable.

In the matter of television, it must be recognized that we often get the programmes we deserve! It is a public service, and it takes the tastes and demands of its audience into account. As clients, we definitely have the right and even the duty to express our opinion over what is shown.

A prominent journalist who was invited to a Christian seminar emphasized how much *one single letter from a television viewer carried weight in the choosing of programmes.* He encouraged Christians to express their opinions much more.

The media world is often thought of as totally secular and therefore difficult to penetrate. Yet, it would be normal enough to be able to offer children good quality cartoons conveying Christian values. In this area, productions that are committed need the understanding and backing of the Body of Christ; designers and script-writers 'adopted' by churches and Christian businessmen could then be better supported in the audio-visual world.

It is a question of faith: do we believe that it is possible to be the head and not the tail (Deut. 28:13), to be again the salt of the earth, even in the world of media?

There are some private Christian TV networks that have begun to dispel the clouds, such as TVP. in Switzerland, which produces videos for a good part of the French-speaking world. In the United States, there have been national Christian networks set up since the matter arrested the conscience of the Body of Christ, and through faithful intercession.

One of the great spheres of influence in the area of education, where the Church is now struggling to regain lost ground, is the *school.* Supposedly inspired by a philosophy that wanted to be impartial and 'secular', it in fact rejects the idea of God more and more obviously. As for methods of education impregnated with humanism, they fail simply because they do not take into account the fact that sin is rooted in the heart of a child (Prov. 22:15). In some of our cities, pupils go as far as threatening and even attacking teachers who dare to give them poor marks.

In a small Swiss town of seven thousand inhabitants, the teachers organized a meeting for the parents, with the theme, 'How do we regain authority over the children?'. With the present methods of education, extracting obedience becomes a real power struggle, and nervous depression is one of its most common results.

In the last few years private Christian schools have multiplied. In Lausanne, a couple from YWAM launched a small primary school. Now, after four years, its number of pupils is coming close to one hundred (from three to eleven years old), and a secondary school level is being planned. The curriculum includes worship, intercession and Bible knowledge and, while all the normal subjects are covered, they are inspired by a Christian philosophy. The parents, some of whom are not believers, scramble to get their children registered there, even though in doing so they are required to give their full agreement to the curriculum!

The real issue, however, is not just to set up a similar system, but to reconquer the sphere of education. In countries like Togo, Burkina Faso and Ivory Coast, the best schools – those who obtain the highest rate of scholastic success – are the private Protestant schools. The result of this is that the majority of government ministers and distinguished officials enrol their children in these schools, who are then often converted during their school years.

No, the battle is not lost, it has just begun, for the present system has started to realize the extent of the problem and is becoming more open to new solutions.

E) Attacks Against The Family

In the United States, one third of marriages end in divorce, while in the same country, among families who read the Bible and confess Jesus as Lord, the statistics are one divorce for every thousand marriages.

Georges Ansermin, a child evangelist and father of three little ones himself, emphasizes that the two pillars of family training are *love* and *firmness*. When a child is receiving affection and correction, he blossoms in the secure environment they create.

Because of the *collapse of the family unit*, these are the two foundations of upbringing that are often absent. We live in a society in which the principles of the Creator are deliberately undermined for the sake of its humanist principles.

'In France, the downfall of fathers was set in motion twenty years ago. On June 4th, 1970, two years after the May '68 youth proclaimed the death of the father, the law marked the end of their privilege by dethroning them from their positions as 'heads of the family.' The idea of paternal power is definitively replaced by that of parental authority, and henceforth restricted to equality of the father and mother. A revolution.' (Extract from the *Express* of June 20th, 1990, from 'The Father-Mother Duel', an article on the family.)

As a result of this dismembering of the family, it is not rare to find a child with two 'mothers' or several 'fathers', which understandably leads to confusion as far as his *identity* is concerned, for he no longer knows to whom he belongs.

It often happens that deep within himself he believes it is 'his fault' and feels responsible for his parents' conflict. False guilt is thus added to his insecurity. Such a situation, experienced as rejection, can lead some to scholastic failure, bulimia and anorexia, delinquency, even depression and suicide. Other children may compensate for the sense of rejection by rebelling and refusing all authority, thus manifesting in fact their deep desire to be loved.

Children and adolescents who are locked into their loneliness, their hatred of self and of the world around them, need to receive real love through us. Every warm and welcoming home can sow the love of God and heal numbers of teenagers adrift.

Children's clubs, if they take place in your home or in the open air, facilitate the meeting of the smallest children in the immediate environment,

Witness the little Spanish girl of six who, as a tiny bud of womanhood, had already learnt all the coarse language of those with whom she lived. She began coming regularly to the club we ran in Grasse, in the south of France. She was converted and, to our surprise, without anyone commenting on it, her vocabulary was radically purified, demonstrating to us once again the reality of the presence of Christ in a child.

In children's camps, there is the tremendous advantage of being around the children for several days, which gives time for a clear demonstration of the plan of God, and leads to many sincere conversions.

Today, God is looking for Christians who will not only incarnate the message in their private lives, but will also share the keys with others, pray with couples in difficulty and with disoriented children. Seminars and family camps which concentrate on this theme have proved very successful, and give opportunity for a deep work of God.

9.3. A Prepared Mission Field!

What, then, are the qualities which make a child more receptive to salvation than an adult?

A) Humility

What did Jesus mean when He said, 'Whoever humbles himself like this child is the greatest in the kingdom of heaven'? (Matt. 18:4) Children, humble! Not really, if I listen to their conversations. 'My father, he's the strongest, and he's the most intelligent person in the whole world!' A child can be as proud as a peacock! And yet, Jesus discerned a humility in them that was a key to the Kingdom. 'Unless you change and become like little children, you will never enter the kingdom of heaven.' (Matt. 18:3b)

In fact, a child accepts food, lodging, comfort and education, without any affectation. He lets his needs be known and expects his little person to be taken care of; he *knows* he is dependent. This is a qualification that is indispensable for receiving salvation, which is *given* when we have no way of deserving it.

Such a condition bewilders many adults who find it 'too easy'! The truth is that it is much too humiliating and mortifying for our ego: if only we could do something to earn it!

B) Malleability

For the teacher, the heart of a child is like a vase of potter's clay, on which anything you wish can be engraved. But for those with a memory, it is like granite, and what is engraved remains... If you visit residents of old people's homes, you will discover that childhood memories are sometimes the only ones that are still alive.

A Christian leader wrote on this subject: 'Childhood is the age of learning. It is an age full of questions. The mind is never as alive, nor the memory as faithful, as in that period. It has been said that a child of seven has already received three quarters of his education. It is the time to teach him eternal truths, and to lead this young life to the Lord.'

Ignatius of Loyola begged, 'Lord, give me the children before they are seven, and afterwards anyone can teach them whatever he wants.'

Why, asks Dutch pastor Herman ter Welle, has the Creator made it possible for a chicken to learn to walk in a matter of a few hours, while it takes a child about a year? Or why is a cat capable of reproducing at one year of age, twelve to fifteen times quicker that a human being? Is it not simply because God wants us to profit from these years, *as a privileged time* for training the future adult? 'Train a child in the way he should go, and when he is old he will not turn from it.' (Prov. 22:6)

It is an urgent mission, for putting off this training until 'later' will often mean 'too late'! An adult hardens himself against the message of the Gospel, whereas a child sometimes makes one think of a sponge, with unlimited capacity! As for the teenager, beneath his closed exterior, he is listening to you attentively, testing you to see if your message is authentic.

Les Compagnons de Daniel (Daniel's Companions) is an organization that informs children of the dangers of drugs well before the real problem of taking them is presented to them. It is during this period, when they are not yet tempted, that they can make an unhurried decision.

C) Trust

A child is naturally trusting; he believes what he is told, and if we do not quench his faith with our adult scepticism, it will move mountains. A witness to this is the true story of a little girl who lived on a farm and loved her cows. One of the animals developed a tumour in its eye, and eventually the veterinarian had to remove the eye. The child was so disturbed by this that each evening she secretly went and prayed for her cow. The vet noticed that something strange was going on in the eye socket of the animal, but left it alone. This cow received a brand new eye! The little girl had not gone to Bible school, but she had a friend called Jesus, and He had created billions of eyes!

D) A Sense Of Justice

Nothing offends a child more than to be unjustly punished! When very small, he already has an acute sense of justice, even if he infringes it, and he spontaneously demands what is right and truthful. I remember hearing of a little girl of five who had just been told the story of the crucifixion. 'It's disgusting what they did to Jesus!' she exclaimed in indignation.

In contrast, the adult has learned to justify his compromises by calling evil good, and to escape truth by relativizing it. Look at Pontius Pilate, who washes his hands and declares in a learned tone, 'What is truth?' All the power of the Holy Spirit is needed to convince the adult of sin, justice and judgement, 'for every year, his unregenerate spirit draws further away from God and becomes less able to receive the truth' (from C.H. Spurgeon).

E) The Need To Be Loved

For the child, it is a *vital necessity* to feel loved. The further the human being grows away from childhood, the more he hardens himself against this throbbing need, but Jesus rejoiced to see that His Father would respond to a sincere, childlike search: 'I praise you

Father, Lord of heaven and earth, because you have hidden these things from the wise and learned, and revealed them to little children.' (Matt. 11:25) Yes, the Father reveals Himself to those who are seeking to be loved and who have not replaced this thirst with pride or glory.

It is reported that in the time of the czars, an experiment was conducted in the nursery attached to a children's orphanage. The little ones received the best nutritional and hygienic care possible, but the nurses were forbidden to hold them. The infant mortality rate was abnormally high in that institution, while elsewhere, where the hygiene was poorer but the human contact much warmer, the children flourished! It is certain that children can simply die when they do not feel loved.

Death may not be physical, but psychic and emotional, when the body is still alive but it is as if the soul is petrified. Dorie, a little American girl at the turn of the century, grew up in an orphanage and was in this condition. When she was twelve she heard the Good News for the first time, but sat like ice throughout this message that was too beautiful to be true! However, something in the sincerity of the person's voice moved her... And if it was true...? So she spoke directly to her Creator,

"God, if you want me, you can have me." Immediately, the power of His love filled her being, and never left her again. Some years later, she married and went out as a missionary to a tribe who had never heard the message of the Gospel.

9.4 A Mission Whose Fruit Remains

'Oh yes, they're very receptive, but it doesn't last!' We sometimes hear remarks like this concerning work among children.

Yet, a survey checking the age at which English-speaking missionaries had been converted was very revealing. The conversions were:

- 75% in childhood
- 19% in adolescence
- 6% only, in adulthood

Yes, by the grace of God, 'the imprint stays', and bears fruit! Some thirtyfold, some sixtyfold, some a hundredfold...

'Without a vision the people perish,' Scripture tells us. It could be paraphrased thus: 'If the Church does not have vision for the children, they will perish.'

We were rather sceptical in 1988 when Loren Cunningham, founder of Youth With A Mission, launched the idea of a million adolescents running with a torch to testify to their missionary commitment. We were only too aware of the enormous logistic work such a project would involve; it was a fine idea, but impossible! Yet the goal was not only reached, it was passed...

9.5 A Mission Where There is Room for Everyone

At present, only 6% of all missionary forces are working among two billion three hundred million human beings!

Since almost half the world's population is under twenty years old, Loren Cunningham proposed that half of his organization should one day be working among the very young. Why not? We need men of faith such as him, for it is they who remind us that nothing is impossible for our God.

It is such a vast field, and there is room for you! Even if you can do no more than pray, your participation is highly valued. 'Ask the Lord of the harvest, therefore, to send out workers into his harvest field.' (Luke 10:2)

It is a tremendous work, to which the Lord encourages us to commit our hearts, our finances, our structures, our strength and our intercession.

You will lose neither your time nor your reward, for 'whatever you did for one of the least of these brothers of mine, you did for me' (Matt. 25:40).

DETACHABLE PAGE TO RECORD
PERSONAL REFLECTION

Summary of chapter IX, A Plea For The Small Half Of The World

- The child is *the world of tomorrow*. He is the target of *attacks* at the level of his existence (abortion), his body, his education, his faith and his family. God is looking for determined disciples who will act according to His Word.

- The child is *predisposed* to receive Christ because of his humility, his receptive character, his simple faith, his sense of justice and his need to be loved. Let us not wait, but teach them from today on, in order to bring them to salvation.

- It is *a fruit that remains*: 75% of missionaries were converted during childhood.

- Children represent *almost half of the world's population*, but only a tiny percentage of Christian workers are involved with them.

- We need vision to regain the lost ground that surrounds the child: family, school, media, social laws.

In what area of my life can the Lord use me to serve His purposes for children?

1. Hospitality?_____

2. Club?_____

3. Education?_____

4. Social help?_____

5. Fight against abortion?_____

6. Help to parents?_____

What part of my prayer life will I commit to this?_____

_____

_____

Am I called?

1. To take part directly in work among children?

_____

_____

2. To support these ministries?_____

_____

_____

Chapter X
Questions And Objections

The pages of this book are intended to give an answer to the nine questions and remarks listed below. In this last chapter, I deal with other questions and considerations often presented, in relation to the subjects already treated. Readers are welcome to write to us if they so wish, with their own questions and considerations. They could well become part of a future edition.

1. *The world is sick; has God let go the controls?*

See chapter I

2. *Is it possible to have close fellowship with God and a real understanding of His will for my life?*

See chapter II

3. *My prayer life is wretched, and I feel God has so much more to teach me...*

See chapter III

4. *I've prayed for my family's conversion for years, but nothing has changed...*

See chapter IV

5. *I know that I should evangelize, but the methods I have heard about seem too aggressive, unsuited to me, or just for the specialists.*

See chapter V

6. *I don't know how to have a good conversation. Sometimes I'm at the table with someone and I have the feeling that all I can do is keep quiet or just say banal things.*

See chapter VI

7. *I'd love to lead certain people to the Lord, but I don't know how to do it.*

See chapter VII

8. *We do a lot of evangelism, but our church doesn't grow. Why not?*

See chapter VIII

9. *The upcoming generation scares me. Is there still hope for a change?*

See chapter IX

• *For us, it's quality at which we're aiming; – quantity is not important!*

This type of reasoning is very common and even much admired, but is it biblical? God considered that all of His creations, including Adam and Eve, were 'very good' (quality), and that is why He commanded growth and multiplication (quantity).

The good seed (quality), Jesus tells us, is the one which multiplies (quantity).

Timothy was encouraged to be an example (quality) for all the faithful (quantity).

Heaven will be filled with a multitude of creatures to the glory of God.

Quality is therefore not an end in itself, but a means to quantity. Quality and quantity are like two sisters, not two rivals or enemies. To choose between one or the other is not only anti-biblical, but dangerous to the growth of the Church and the Kingdom of God. It is also sometimes selfish: 'We do so well between us.'

A large crowd is not, in itself, proof of divine blessing and approval, but neither are sparsely populated pews and absenteeism.

A remark often heard being inferred from this reasoning, and which also deserves examination in the light of the Bible, is the following:

• *Spiritual revival will sweep away organization, planning and timetables, and vice versa.*

When Jesus multiplied the loaves and fishes, there were not people left hungry on one side and people filled on the other. Why not? Because He had taken care to have the crowd sit down in groups of fifty and a hundred (Mark 6:39-40). The Lord organized that meal in such a way that there was quality and quantity.

The first local church, in Jerusalem, quickly grew to five thousand families. At the time of this powerful revival, seven men filled with the Holy Spirit were chosen by the apostles to organize the distribution of food (Acts 6:1-8).

It is essential that we understand this principle: the Holy Spirit is not overwhelmed by quantity. It is indispensable if we want to see our cities transformed, and that will require us to be organized. Pastor Y. Cho's church meets in groups of fifty thousand people (because of the size of the building), which means there are seven consecutive services each Sunday. (Seven groups of fifty thousand also come to midweek meetings) To the visitor, one of the most striking characteristics of the church is the rapidity, calm and order with which these rotations take place.

The growth of your church and revival in your city will, sooner or later, require the Christians to drop the false quality-quantity duality and accept that the Holy Spirit is the generator of order and harmony, while still preserving liberty and creativity.

Any effective organization aims simultaneously at quality and quantity; must Christians be the last to understand this? Take the example of ten thousand children needing a cholera vaccination within two weeks. Choosing between quality and quantity would put their lives in danger. It would simply be acting with maturity to organize ten thousand vaccines, ten thousand syringes and the necessary number of nurses according to our means. God does not expect less from His ambassadors.

- *I don't have a ministry.*

Jesus said, 'I tell you the truth, anyone who has faith in me will do what I have been doing. He will do even greater things that these...' (John 14:12). Few verses have been more misused than this one. Look at what we all too often make Him say, which does not in fact correspond to Jesus' words:

1) 'He who has faith in Me will do greater works than I do.' Many mention particular 'great works', which today amount to things like preaching on the radio or TV, opening a Christian hospital, or travelling across the world, while they freely, or deliberately, ignore the first part of the promise. Doing greater works does not in the least exempt us from doing *those that He did!*

2) 'He who has faith in Me will also do works that I did if he lives in the time of the first apostles.' The underlying interpretation is that the true spiritual gifts were only for that epoch.

3) 'He who has faith in Me will do only the works that his denomination plans.' In fact the Bible was not inspired and given in order to defend our doctrines, but to correct them.

4) 'Those called to be 'great' evangelists, prophets, pastors, teachers or apostles will do the works that I do and will do great things.' This is the credo of Christians who do not accept that their first call, the very reason for their existence, is not to receive this or that ministry, but to become like Jesus. Not a poetic, sentimental or imaginary, 'effeminate guru' type of Jesus, but the real Jesus of the Gospel, who said:

'Go back and report to John what you have seen and heard: the blind receive sight, the lame walk, those who have leprosy are cured, the deaf hear, the dead are raised, and the good news is preached to the poor.' (Luke 7:22) This is how Jesus Himself describes His works (cf. Luke 13:32, 4:18-21).

Supposing, then, that you do not have one of those five ministries, I encourage you to consider the promise of Jesus, that if you have faith in Him *you will do* the works that He has done, and even greater works, for it is He, and not a weak, changing, 'adjusted' or partial Jesus, Who *lives in you!*

• *I don't even pray as I should for my neighbours, so how can I pray for the nations?*

Praying in ever-increasing concentric circles may appear logical, but it is not biblical. I doubt that you will manage a worthwhile prayer life by 'obliging' the Holy Spirit to come into your dimensions, yet, unconsciously, that is what you would rather like. On the contrary, it is by allowing God to lead you into His dimensions that you will pray effectively for yourself, your family, your neighbours, your church. The prayer life of the smallest Christian can be universal, for it is to the God of the universe that he says, 'Father, teach me to pray according to Your will, that Your Kingdom will come, that Your will will be done *on earth* as it is in heaven.'

• *Is it really worth undertaking long-term projects, when Jesus is going to come back in the next few years?*

If we continually have the underlying wish that Jesus will return in the next ten or fifteen years at the latest, we will cause many young people with a promising career to choose shorter training, transitory jobs, short-term projects. If in 1973 you had suggested that Christ would perhaps not have come back by 1991, in many circles you would have been accused of unbelief or of being a wet blanket. Has that situation really changed now?

Is there not at the root of all that a subtle form of pride, that all the end-time prophecies must be absolutely fulfilled in our own lifetime?

Too many Christians have fallen into this trap, imagining they have received revelation from the Lord that He will indeed return while they themselves are still alive! When, for example, a twenty-four year old makes such a statement before a bunch of newly converted teenagers, three conclusions can be drawn: either Christ 'must' return in the immediate future, or this man is immortal, or he is wrong! Such experiences that I have known have fallen into the third category.... This way of thinking leads some Christians into 'recognizing' fulfilment of prophecies in every contemporary event. Even if they have never prophesied in their own church, they comment on the smallest international conference in a way that Elijah and Elisha would have hesitated to do!

An honest reading of the New Testament shows us that the apostles themselves had not imagined that the Lord could prolong His grace for more than nineteen centuries (cf. 1 John 2:18). He is still sovereign. Wait faithfully on the Lord every day, for the Spirit, in us, says to Him, 'Come,' but let us also have the courage and humility to play our role fully today, as if we are but a tiny link in the long history of the Church. Failing to do this, Christians risk forming a subculture which lives for the temporary, leaving our societies to fall deeper into darkness, and thus losing the salt that our predecessors poured out at the cost of their lives. It is true that the signs of the times are changing, and the Bridegroom is at the door. May He find us sober and active, not investing a few years, but our whole lives, for the salvation of as many as possible. 'Let us run with perseverance the *race [career]* marked out for us. Let us fix our eyes on Jesus...' (Heb. 12:1-2).

- *Isn't the time for big evangelism campaigns over?*

No, but we can learn from our brothers and sisters of other countries, continents and denominations what will make them fruitful. To state the contrary when we live in the time of the greatest campaigns in all history is, at the least, regrettable. Putting the individual witness and large campaigns in opposition to one another is to ignore the fact that the individual witness is increased tenfold by the impetus of the large effort, and that the latter is effective through the multitude of individual witnesses!

- *Isn't it misplaced spending to use so much money for an evangelism campaign?*

I have never heard the devil protest against an immoral film that costs three times the sum of a campaign, or against drug trafficking, which in Switzerland alone is valued between five hundred million and three and a half billion Swiss francs per year, or yet against buying a fighter jet costing a hundred million francs, which would be enough for a thousand evangelism campaigns of large proportions!

In fact, sin costs forty billion dollars per day in our societies around the world! But protests on the subject are very quiet...

No, it would be folly to excuse ourselves from giving our money to fight against all forms of evil and to spread life and salvation freely through the Gospel.

- *Shouldn't we promote local ministries, rather than invite preachers in from the other side of the world?*

How many committees lose precious years over this kind of debate! Others compare the merits of adult evangelism to that of children; others, decentralized evangelism by neighbourhoods to a large, centralized effort by everyone; yet others compare the merits of the one-on-one contacts of each Christian to bringing in an evangelist, etc..

In these debates, everyone is certain that he is right, whereas the difficulty rests simply in the fact that all are right. The real error is in comparing things that the Holy Spirit deems to be complementary, because we can be sure that His intention is to promote local ministries *as much as* international ones, for He has raised up both of them. He wants to save adults *and* children, and not choose between the two. His aim is to reach our neighbourhoods, but *also* to touch the whole city and to thus bless our unity demonstrated in these bigger gatherings. He desires *each* Christian to be a source of salvation, and that is why He sends *evangelists* who will not only explain how to do it, but who will live it out before their very eyes! In the coming years, why not use all these possibilities, not uselessly comparing them, but combining them intelligently in an exercise that will bear fruit?

• *How do I organize follow-up if I lead an evangelism trip to China (or a similar situation)?*

This question, which a School of Evangelism leader in Lausanne asked concerning an actual case, in fact fits many situations which are less complicated but where follow-up work is, nevertheless, almost non-existent. Your travel budget is going to be high. Since one of your goals is the salvation of Chinese people, it is normal to invest in the follow-up. You could take five little transistor radios in your luggage with directions on how to get frequencies for Christian broadcasts in Mandarin. You could also take Bibles and other literature in the language, and find out if there are Bible courses available. If there is a mail service, you could also ask the students to each correspond with a few students who speak English. Before leaving on the trip, ask the people expecting you there what you can do to help them with this specific goal. Work in as close collaboration as possible with the local Christians and entrust them with the newborn babes. In conclusion, let us emphasize that it is always possible to prepare well; it takes time, finances, initiative and discernment in prayer, but God will always be faithful to lead those who want to take care of the new converts.

• *Our youth group, our local or national church, are not ready for evangelism.*

What are you doing to change the situation? Who could help you? Are you aware that even young Christians who evangelize grow much more quickly that those who are coaxed along and even 'nursed' for years? Has God not placed someone among you who has the gift to initiate others into witnessing? Whatever the case, do not allow the situation to become fossilized; too many *movements* have become *monuments* today because they 'were not ready' – from one generation to the next!

• *God has shown me that before evangelizing we must first prepare ourselves – sanctify ourselves – be healed – buy a sound system – sell the sound system – get to know each other better – practise more – be more... be less...* The list is endless.

These arguments paralyse a large part of the Lord's army, and Satan probably holds the absolute record of things to do 'before' evangelizing and he will issue them generously to any who might be missing some! How do we recognize the true preparation of the Holy

Spirit as opposed to seductive and paralysing arguments? By examining the fruit.

Some will always be talking about getting prepared, but in an abstract way, without ever fixing goals or dates or making plans. Twenty years later, their conversation has not changed; they still want 'first' to... 'before' evangelizing. As Jesus emphasized, not only do they lead no one into the Kingdom of God, but they prevent those who want to do it from beginning.

In contrast, there are others who organize actively, and some time later the preparation has turned into action and fruit begins to appear.

- *I don't evangelize, but I train others to do it.*

If this is the case, you are training people who will not evangelize! Who you are and what you do influences your disciples much more than what you say. *They will suppose that he who does not evangelize is,* like their teacher or leader, *wiser, more spiritual, greater* than he who 'wastes' his time 'directly' evangelizing. Your 'disciple' will say to himself, 'Why should I evangelize? It's so much more effective to train others to do it...' Jesus was the best educator and the greatest spiritual leader that the world has ever known, and He trained His disciples by being the Friend of sinners. You are not greater than Him.

To train others to evangelize without doing it yourself is as much a deception as trying to train a parachutist without ever jumping yourself, or giving a swimming lesson without ever getting wet!

- *The world's population is growing so rapidly, how much time would be needed to proclaim the Gospel to everyone, assuming it can be done?*

It is estimated that at present there are more than half a billion committed Christians in the world. If we suppose that each one of them leads just one person a year to Christ, the growth rate would be as follows:

$$\begin{aligned}
\text{January } 1993 &= 500{,}000{,}000 \\
\text{January } 1994 &= 1{,}000{,}000{,}000 \\
\text{January } 1995 &= 2{,}000{,}000{,}000 \\
\text{January } 1996 &= 4{,}000{,}000{,}000 \\
\text{January } 1997 &= 8{,}000{,}000{,}000
\end{aligned}$$

But as there will not even be that number of human beings on earth in 1997, the Christians will not all be able to lead one person to Christ, nor even proclaim the Gospel for the first time to someone!

Obviously, things are not as simple as that, for linguistic, cultural, spiritual and geo-political barriers are very real. However, it is good to take note of these numbers, for if every disciple of Christ led someone to conversion between the first of January and the thirty-first of December, the world would be transformed.

For centuries, Christians have obeyed the Master's command without realizing what it actually meant. Take the example of Bible translation. We know today that there are about six thousand languages spoken around the globe, and the Scriptures exist, at least partially, in more than two thousand of them (generally in the principal languages).

Linguists spend an average of eight years from their first entry into a new tribe to the printing of several, if not all, the books of the Bible. (They simultaneously teach a number of the indigenous people to read.) A new translation of the New Testament comes out every fortnight. If this rate accelerates, it is not impossible that the Word of God will be available in every language in a dozen or so more years.

But the evangelization of our entire planet therefore depends mainly on the Church, that is, on you and me.

- *Can we really hope one day to see certain nations becoming followers of Christ?*

Several servants of God believe that the Lord will enable this to happen, one reason being that He commanded it Himself (Matt. 28:20) and asked us to pray for it, and another that some nations will at least serve as witnesses to the others. We therefore need to grasp two things:

1) In a 'disciple' nation, every person will keep his freedom of choice as to his salvation, and so will not necessarily be converted, but the laws, justice, education, social relations, culture, media, etc., will be thoroughly impregnated with the Word and will seek to glorify Christ. Certain areas and cities have already experienced this in the course of past centuries in times of powerful moves of repentance, such as the Rochester revival, mentioned in chapter I, when eighty percent of the population was profoundly converted (see also Acts 9:34-35). Let us remember, too, that if the South Korean revival continues at its present rate, three quarters of the population could be born again by approximately the year 2000.

2) Just as any disciple of Christ, despite a sanctified life, can break a leg, have cavities in his teeth, make a mistake, sin and repent,

fall sick and grow old, so will a nation not be a paradise, even though it is submitted to Christ in all essential areas! Evangelization and revival will never replace the return of Jesus Christ and the establishment of His Kingdom!

Certainly in these nations there will be glorious transformations, fearing God alone will lead to security, faithfulness, dignity, joy, trust and so many other benefits to which political systems aspire but do not know the key. But these nations will not thus be sheltered from bad choices, and nor will their drivers, which will still mean accidents, hospitalizations, sometimes deaths. People will continue to grow old and die. There will still be disappointments, tears, questions; it will still be necessary to repent and ask for the grace of God.

Let us look at an example on a smaller scale. Some local churches who experience revival confuse walking in the Spirit with life in heaven: when someone is about to die, they pray as if the fact of being filled with the Holy Spirit will assure us of immortality. They can thus experience some bitter disappointments (in spite of magnificent healings and miracles), and some will reject prayer for the sick, or will become divided on this question, at the risk of losing everything.

Let us not confuse the life of the disciple (individually and collectively) in this present world with heaven! When a nation is a disciple of Christ, it will resemble a society of disciples with innumerable blessings, but it will still be on this earth...

- *Will we remember our earthly life in eternity?*

This question has a certain importance because it in fact examines the connection between our personality and the character of God. While respecting differing opinions, my answer is yes, for the following reasons:

1) The rich man and Lazarus remembered perfectly (Luke 16:19-31).

2) All the human beings playing a role in Revelation seem to remember their life here below very well.

3) All the people who come back to life, medically or miraculously, and who remember what happened beyond, report that they were well aware of who they were and their memory was not affected.

180

4) We shall be eternally grateful for our salvation, and we shall know why Jesus has nail-pierced hands.

5) How could we worship God for His justice without remembering the facts?

6) Would we even be aware of who we are without that capacity?

7) Biblical happiness has nothing to do with something magic, a drug, or some manipulation of our personality. On the contrary, it is founded on truth, wisdom, knowledge, justice, forgiveness, love; such happiness is real. God will therefore not have to 'modify' an aspect of our being in order to make our joy perfect. He Himself will be perfectly happy with a faultless memory, even though He chooses to forget confessed sin. We shall be in His image.

- *In wanting to take an interest in the whole world, isn't there a danger of falling into an unhealthy, one-world philosophy, New Age or the world government of the anti-Christ?*

Who is the imitator of whom? What would we think of someone who refused to exhibit the painting of a master for fear that people would think it was a forgery, or who would refuse to wear a diamond because fake ones look real? Yes, at times some of us hold to this kind of argument, but it comes from an attitude of retreat that neither Jesus nor the apostles taught. The anti-Christ will institute a world government imitating the Kingdom of God. Failing to prepare, love, live and proclaim this universal Kingdom would be unqualifiable error before the splendour of the King of kings!

- *Isn't Christianity bound to be in a minority?*

No, for in His Word God calls all humanity to Himself (John 12:32). If disciples are in the minority, the responsibility for it rests with man, but it is not fatal. God acts, within the limits of His wisdom, His love and the free will He has given us (and which makes us human beings), to reconcile all men to Himself. This said, let us emphasize two aspects which are fundamental to this question.

1) The true disciple is faithful, not because Christ is popular (or unknown), but for love of Him and for the truth.

2) The value of the Kingdom of God is intrinsic; it will never be sold off or its requirements diluted, even if the whole of humanity rebelled against it.

God's desire expressed through the prophets who forewarned humanity of Jesus' sacrifice, the missionary command, the conquering spirit of the first Christians, the promise of the latter rains, the final, glorious Church, and the multitude that no one can count worshipping God in heaven, give no room for a demobilizing pessimism.

We are experiencing the greatest harvest in all history, as thirty-five people are converted to Jesus Christ every minute, which means more than two thousand every hour! And that number is growing.

The real question, mentioned in chapter III, is this: in the face of lost humanity, am I inspired by the spirit of Jonah, or by that of the apostles? A carnal prophet announces judgement and rubs his hands, but a true prophet announces destruction while weeping and hoping that the sinner will repent and live.

'"Do I take any pleasure in the death of the wicked?" declares the Sovereign Lord. "Rather, am I not pleased when they turn from their ways and live?"' (Ezek. 18:23)

- *How does one maintain the balance between compassion and evangelism?*

The Bible presents us with a 'two-handed' evangelism, one hand bringing the Word (proclamation), the other bringing healing compassion (social). It is difficult to maintain the balance. Some missionary hospitals have succeeded, and thousands of sick have received the Gospel. Others have been swallowed by the tyranny of the urgent, and no longer see conversions, even though that was their first calling. One of the causes, which you have perhaps experienced yourself, is that we may begin with a fine and effective two-handed evangelism, but slide imperceptibly toward a two-man evangelism (for example, we appoint an evangelist in order to 'free' the nurse), then we create two departments (the care section and the witnessing section), which evolve into two institutions (the hospital and the church). At this stage, in too many cases we end up with two enemies, strong on their own rights: 'Why do you come and upset 'our' sick people?'

It is true that we are one body with different functions, but in one's life and profession, it is not possible to separate these two elements, any more than a man can say to his wife, 'From now on, you read the Bible and I'll pray,' or, 'You eat and I'll drink!'

- *Isn't there a danger of manipulating people when trying to ask them good questions?*

Yes, just as there is a danger of food poisoning if you eat, or a car accident if you drive. But something is not bad in itself simply because it carries a risk factor. To be aware of possible slips should keep us on guard against them. Asking good questions can positively influence all your contacts, so do not refrain, but rather, do it with wisdom and for the good of your neighbour.

In conclusion, a significant number of questions find their answers in statistics.

I have selected one hundred statistics here out of three thousand (the year of reference being 1990 unless otherwise stated). They are often full of significance and, I hope, will prove very useful to you in understanding the needs of our world and in praying with knowledge and awareness.

Gospel and world population:

Daily number of births world-wide	388,000
People newly evangelized daily	364,000
Daily personal conversions	50,000
Annual number of births	141.6 million
People newly evangelized annually	133.0 million
New Christians per year (all denominations)	65.1 million
Less Christians per year (deaths, defections)	26.4 million
Net Christian growth per year	38.7 million
People born since AD 33 (Pentecost)	34.90 billion
People evangelized since AD 33	13.10 billion
Christians since AD 33	8.29 billion
% of people evangelized since AD 33	38%
% of people now being evangelized	76.3%

The Bible:

Access to Scripture in mother tongue	world pop. 92%
Annual distribution of Scripture portions	1.43 billion
Languages having at least one book of Bible	over 2,000
New translations of Scripture in progress	over 820
Total number of languages (+ or - according to dialects)	5,600

Evangelism through radio and television:

Christian broadcasts in mother tongue	world pop. 86.5%
Believers contacted solely via radio/TV	20 million
Number converted annually via radio/TV	3 million
Number converted daily via radio/TV	8,220

Missionary forces:

'Full-time' Christians	4.2 million
Expatriate career missionaries	285,250
Expatriate short-term missionaries	180,000
Expatriate Pentecostal/charismatic missionaries	85,000
Expatriate Pent./char. missionaries by AD 2000	167,000
Pentecostal/charismatic members (all leanings)	372.65 million
Pentecostal/charismatic members by AD 2000	562.52 million
Main Christian confessions	90
Total number of Christian denominations	23,500
Secret believers	137 million
Christian worship venues (not including prayer groups)	2.6 million
Disciples participating in Great Commission	500 million
Daily prayer cells	10 million
Jesus film seen by	380 million
Large-scale evangelism campaigns per year	2,500
Total daily giving per parishioner	1.85 dollars
Daily giving per parishioner for missions	0.1 dollar

Christian population: (*all leanings*)	in AD 1900	in AD 2000
Europe	278,000,000	429,000,000
Africa	10,000,000	390,000,000
Asia, ex-USSR, Oceania	129,000,000	368,000,000
North America	79,000,000	255,000,000
Latin America	59,000,000	565,000,000
Totals	558,000,000	2,020,000,000

Religious affiliation:

Christians (1992, E. European changes not	1,837 million

included)

Muslims	935 million
Hindus	705 million
Buddhists	323 million
Jews	18 million

Problems, vices, sins:

Abortions per year	65 million
People involved in drug trafficking	40 million
Murder victims per year	850,000
Suicides per year	401,000
Smokers	650 million
Annual deaths connected with tobacco	2.6 million
Annual deaths due to polluted water	9.1 million
Annual deaths due to malaria	5 million
Abused women	200 million
Children with no family	300 million
People with no shelter/home	100 million
People sexually abused during childhood	200 million
Homosexuals	80 million
Lesbians	30 million
Female prostitutes	20 million
Male prostitutes	2 million
Torture practised in	110 countries
Christian martyrs since AD 33	40.7 million
Christian martyrs since 1950	9.96 million
Slaves, forced labourers	32 million
Annual military expenditure	$950 billion
Annual cost for sin structure	$5,200 billion

Miscellaneous:

Married couples	800 million
Unmarried couples	650 million
percentage of world's work done by women	62%
Income earned by women	10%
Property owned by women	1%
Literate adults of world population	71%
Literate Christian adults	88%
Christian secondary schools	45,000

Average annual income per family	13,070 dollars
Average annual income per non-Christian	1,350 dollars
Average annual income per Christian	5,510 dollars
Cities with more than one million inhabitants	330
Average age of world population	24.4 years
Average life span of world population	62.3 years
Children under 15 years	32% of world pop.
People with English as mother tongue	400 million
English speakers	1,100 million
Chinese speakers	1,000 million
Spanish speakers	450 million
French speakers	380 million

EUROPE

AFRICA

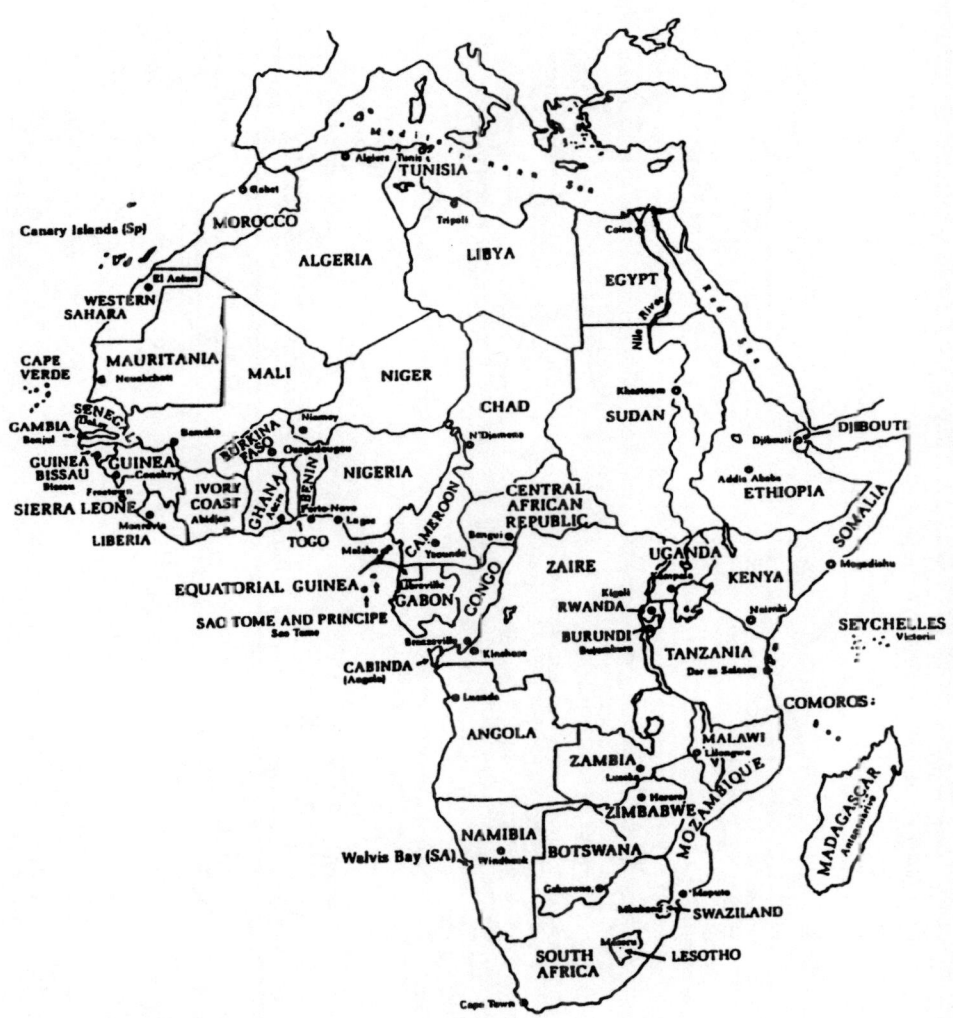

ASIA

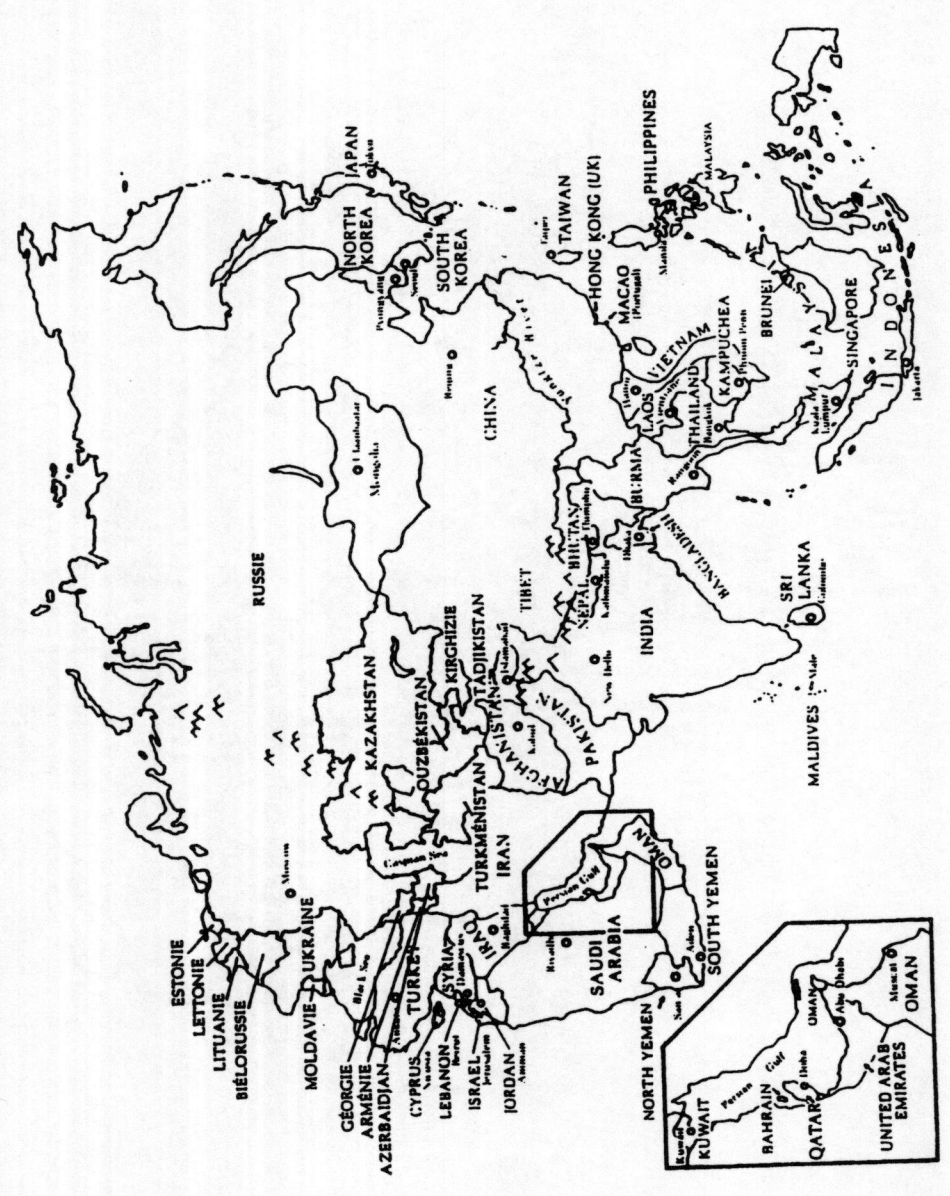

OCEANIA

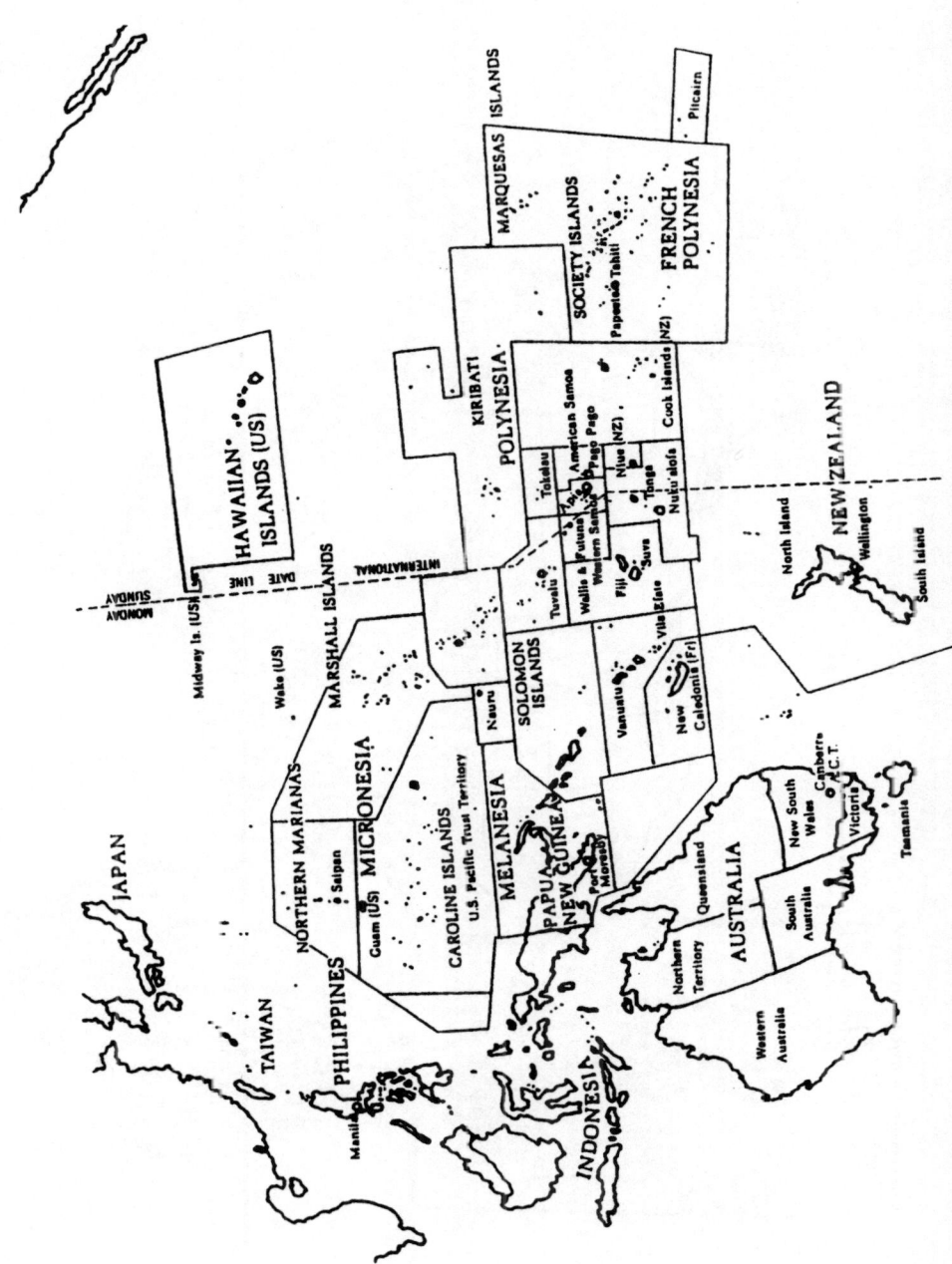

NORTH AMERICA

SOUTH AMERICA

Letter To The Reader

Dear reader,

Thank you for the interest you have taken in this book. Our hope is that after examining all things in the light of Scripture, the nine detachable pages will accompany your reflection and become reality.

God is raising up millions of harvesters today, fervent in prayer, fervent in spreading the Gospel. He is calling you, too, right where you are. Believe in His call, for your response to it is as precious in His eyes as that of the twelve first disciples.

This book, as with the preceding one, *Messengers of Life*, can be taught in the form of a seminar open to everybody. However, we want evangelism to be kept the priority. If you would like to invite us to your country or area, feel free to write to us, taking into consideration the two following requests:

– Is it possible to assemble the greatest possible number of Christians of your area, in order to avoid repeating the same thing in the same place, one year later?

– Can you organize, simultaneously with or following the seminar, an evangelism campaign, so the same Christians will be able to put into practice what they hear?

May the Lord of Life lead you in moving ahead with Him, whether in your hidden prayer ministry or in public witnessing, that His will may be done, and that the greatest possible number will be saved.

May He bless you and encourage you on the way!

Carlo and Michèle Brugnoli
I. de Montolieu 79
CH - 1010 Lausanne
SWITZERLAND

Translating *Catch The Vision of God*

We are very interested in having this book translated and edited in Spanish, Portuguese or other languages. If you are able to help us in any way with this, please contact us. Thank you.

Translations exist in:

- *French*
Progresser Avec Dieu
Edition Jeunesse en Mission
La Maison
CH 1261 Burtigny
SWITZERLAND

- *German*
Erzalt Es Allen Volkern
Edition Projektion J Verlag
Niederwaldstrasse 14
D - W - 6200 Wiesbaden
GERMANY

- *Italian*
Progredire Con Dio
Edition Uomini Nuovi
I - 21030 marchirolo (VA)
ITALY

194

Quotations

Chapter III

Extract quoted, with permission, from *Luis Palau* by Jerry B Jenkins.

Chapter VII

Extract quoted, with permission, from the tract, *Assurance of Salvation* by Billy Graham.

All Bible quotations are taken from the New International version, unless otherwise stated.